Farming Cuba

D1573270

FARM
ING
CUBA

**URBAN
AGRICULTURE
FROM THE
GROUND UP**

Carey Clouse

Princeton Architectural Press, New York

Contents

Intro-
duction

AS THE ENDING OF AN ERA OF CHEAP OIL THREATENS GLOBAL food security and forces a reexamination of food-production techniques, alternative models for self-sufficiency demand our attention. City dwellers—in the United States and abroad— have launched a cultural conversation around their relationship to food systems, and in so doing have helped to expose the social and environmental deficiencies implicit in large-scale food production. Many of these activists also see direct engagement as a means of ensuring responsible food security and have welcomed agricultural processes back into the city—as had been the case in urban environments such as Machu Picchu and ancient Egypt—in an effort to better control and understand their own foodsheds. In this context, innovative urban design interventions incorporating productive uses for vacant and underused land offer inspiring blueprints for a post-oil future.

This kind of spatial economy is well underway in Cuba, the socialist nation long burdened by U.S. trade embargoes and the dissolution of the Soviet bloc in 1989. Cuba's isolation from international trade ushered in a new era: the return of locavorism and a willful resurrection of the island's foodshed. This self-reliance led to a new brand of Cuban sustainability— one born out of necessity and fueled by the people.

In the face of resource scarcity, Cubans responded by rethinking land use, implementing organic farming practices, developing low-input agricultural systems, and honing techniques for independence on an island without oil. A rush of socialist success stories followed suit, highlighting innovation sparked by food, fuel, and tool shortages. The government embraced urban agriculture, city dwellers enlisted in the effort, and the island began to provide for itself. As a result, Cuba has emerged as a world leader in sustainable agricultural practices, central to which is a flourishing urban farming program.

During the course of the last twenty-five years of urban farming in Havana, a wide variety of design strategies and physical characteristics have coalesced to form this robust food security initiative. Socialist Cuba's economical and functional methods could be readily applied to other post-oil environments, providing a set of deployable techniques for the food landscapes of cities around the globe. These innovative urban design interventions—tested over decades and appropriate for underused urban spaces—provide a new model for bolstering food production while reducing dependence on oil.

While historically the "agrarian and the urban are two categories of thought that have more often than not been opposed to one another," they necessarily commingle under the threat of resource scarcity.[1] In the Cuban context, urban agriculture tends toward functional motivations rather than aesthetic considerations. However, the divide between conceptions of formal design and utilitarian objectives could be reduced—or even eliminated—by integrating designers into the planning process. In claiming urban farming as a critical piece of "the Future City," the international design community has an opportunity to "grapple with the implications for urban form attendant to their renewed interest in the agricultural."[2] And in the disciplines of architecture, landscape architecture, and urban planning— as well as in the global consciousness—topics of self-sufficiency and food production promise to assume new forms and roles.[3]

Landscape Urbanism

Havana's food system begins with a series of land-use strategies that occupy the intersection of policy and urban form. The infrastructure that supports this movement lays a common groundwork for food security, establishing a set of rules, a code of ethics, and tiers of engagement. At the root of this framework is a series of farm typologies that forms a kit of parts ready for deployment across an extant urbanized landscape. Cuba's urban food system can be understood as a new photosynthetic infrastructure comprising many distinct pieces that are each contextually responsive and independently activated.

This food network is a clear example of a system's approach to food independence. In this sense the urban agricultural innovations of Cuba are embodied by many of the same infrastructural and social concerns that shaped the landscape urbanism movement that gained momentum in the United States and Europe during the early 2000s. This theoretical reframing has been adopted by many activists in the design community outside of Cuba, whose focus on "urban infrastructure has been repositioned as a topic combining the potential for social and environmental progress, while avoiding the blind alleys and dark corners of urban form."[4] In expanding the profession, landscape architect and professor Charles Waldheim suggests that these issue-oriented urbanists might actually "move the field from its cultural confines into the more quotidian qualities of daily life."[5] Here, the field of landscape urbanism provides a broad platform for the sustainable solutions and systems that do not fall neatly into one of the disparate disciplines of architecture, landscape architecture, and urban planning, and Waldheim's approach launches the conversation into an orbit of broader social relevance.

In identifying Cuba's urban agriculture system as a product of landscape urbanism—rather than the limiting fields of architecture, landscape architecture, or planning—the work can be freed from formal expectations. Although this country-wide initiative lacks design work with a capital D, Cuba's new urban food system offers a sophisticated overarching organizational structure—understood to have emerged informally—that can now be more intentionally co-opted by other countries.

Havana's emergent urban spaces contribute to a new brand of food-centered landscape urbanism, with all of the attendant implications for space and form.

Cuba's vanguard approach to urban agriculture now pairs informal, grassroots participation with official design guidelines and state sponsorship. While this movement began as an unplanned, organic, and spontaneous response to food scarcity in the early 1990s, it has since become absorbed into and formalized by the state. Despite its clear and discernible organization today, this urban foodshed emerged from an iterative decade-long participatory process. The structure of Havana's urban farming network thus developed as a response to existing needs, revealing surprisingly elegant forms and an unusually supportive host state.

In spite of its informal roots, Cuba's urban agriculture response exhibits key indicators of design sophistication. Havana's experiment in self-sufficiency—emphasizing local food, plant, and fuel production—strengthens communities, reduces carbon emissions, and supports biodiversity. This growing infrastructure is an example of what planner and educator Nina-Marie Lister would call *adaptive ecological design*, one that allows for "ecological and programmatic complexity, for both biological and sociocultural diversity, and, accordingly, all facets of sustainability."[6] These agricultural efforts outperform conventional farms and plantations in Cuba, providing a new agricultural typology built upon the leftover scraps of public land found inside the city limits.

Responding to Crisis

Cuba's already-tenuous trade capacity functionally disappeared in 1989 when the island-nation experienced a sudden—and enduring—economic crisis with the collapse of the Soviet Union. The acute resource scarcity that ensued affected both nationally produced and imported food products, and launched the Special Period in Time of Peace: an austerity program that was officially mandated in 1991 and has come to represent the extreme isolation endured by the country during this extended period of economic crisis. Just as author Thomas Friedman was formulating his treatise on global flattening, Cuba withdrew into a remote and inaccessible outpost—a true trade island.[7]

This isolation has now persisted for more than two decades, during which many observers had anticipated Cuba's ruin. Astonishingly, and against all odds, Cuba's state economy has persevered—even as economists and urban theorists have agreed that protracted socioeconomic decay like that experienced by the island "makes urban resilience exceptionally difficult to sustain."[8]

One would expect that such a sudden imposition of great austerity and isolation on a society and economy deeply enmeshed in the web of global commerce would cause its collapse. Scientist and author Jared Diamond identifies this as a common factor of civilization collapse, when through "decreased support by friendly neighbors, [trade partners] can no longer provide the essential import or the cultural tie, [and] your own society may become weakened as a result."[9] As early as 1960, Cuba's trading partners were limited due to the U.S. Cuban Democracy Act, but not until the lucrative trade agreements buoyed by an ideologically aligned Soviet bloc vanished in 1989 was Cuba forced to turn inward. Today, Cuba's self-reliance and radical egalitarianism, which are intentionally disassociated from neocolonial influences of the past, foster an island-wide sense of solidarity.

Cuba's unconventional food landscape offers a perspective that is both cautionary and inspiring. Standing against the backdrop of political and human rights violations, Fidel and Raúl Castro, the two brothers who have governed Cuba since 1959, ultimately rejected Green Revolution principles in favor of a socially- and ecologically-oriented agricultural process. Although Havana's sophisticated system of urban agriculture was not planned at the outset, it fell neatly into the socialist mode of production and received early support from party leaders. Much like the spontaneous urbanism identified by architect Cedric Price, urban planner Peter Hall, writer Paul Barker, and critic Reyner Banham in their groundbreaking article "Non-plan: an experiment in freedom," early growing efforts provided Cuban citizens with an opportunity to relate to food production on their own terms.[10] Originating from desperation and defined by direct engagement, Havana's urban farming represents a people's movement.

Even in a country with a socialist land policy, farming can serve as a visible and physical means of claiming space, and—especially in this context—urban food production remains a "clear way to emphasize one's right to have a say in planning."[11] Guerrilla gardening by city dwellers adopting abandoned urban spaces, for example, presents an opportunity for place-based action and civic improvement. This kind of space hijacking fits squarely into the socialist ethic, specifically when converting commonly held lands into a more productive capacity for all.

The food crisis that followed the events of 1989 brought about an otherwise unimaginable inversion of power, allowing guerrilla growers to operate quasi-capitalist enterprises under the full support of a one-party police state. These allowances by the Cuban government signaled a citizen's occupation of the city, very close to that described by geographer David Harvey in *Rebel Cities: From the Right to the City to the Urban Revolution*; in this case the right "to claim some kind of shaping power over the processes of urbanization, over the ways in which our cities are made and remade, and to do so in a fundamental and radical way."[12] This enlightened attitude toward access and engagement—at least in terms of food production—continues to stand in sharp contrast to corporate agribusiness practices promoted by the United States.

Beyond highlighting one country's response to crisis, this story of resilience charts a course that could feasibly be run again. Using the infrastructure of cities and towns, Cubans discovered "both old and new ways to boost production of basic foods without relying on imports."[13] In doing so, their experience has galvanized a self-sufficiency movement within the country and now provides a model of post-oil food production for other nations. This is the kind of information that could facilitate and encourage other cities or nations to transition. As journalist Bill McKibben notes, if the global foodshed should suddenly seize up, "it's somehow useful to know that someone has already run the experiment."[14]

Resilience

In contrast to the natural systems approach of ecologists— who define resilience in terms of elasticity, or the ability of a post-disaster environment to return to its original state—historian Max Page identifies a type of civic post-crisis resilience that carries productive implications. He describes this as the renewed vitality demonstrated in rebuilding, which implies growth and progress.[15] In the context of Havana's emergent foodshed, this form of resilience, which led to innovation and restructuring, was the only viable option for the country due to the U.S. trade embargo. This approach—critical to the success of the urban agriculture movement in Cuba—created a brand of community-based resilience that embraced both ecological design principles and household food security.

Agriculture's return to the city presents a new urban ecology, one designed to feed people while reinforcing natural processes. In this sense gardens reveal gaps in the urban hardscape—opportunities to engage with sustainability in a context of environmental degradation. Urban naturalist Lyanda Lynn Haupt suggests that societies "use an idea of 'Nature Out There' to ignore [their] ravenous uses of natural resources"; whereas living landscapes within a city can serve as a reminder and a platform for engagement with the natural world.[16] In Havana, nature made visible through the medium of food production promotes broader goals of sustainability and stewardship in what architecture and urban design historian Grahame Shane calls a "new basis of performative urbanism that emerges from the bottom up, geared to the technological and ecological realities of the postindustrial world."[17]

At the urban scale, locally grown food products contribute to self-sufficiency on many fronts, not the least of which is giving individuals a measure of control over their own sustenance. Urban gardens offer a logical, affordable, and accessible link between farm and table, bolstering food autonomy from the scale of the household up to the regional foodshed. This is a ground-up movement in which growers have the power to choose the food they produce, the seeds they save, and the land they cultivate, and consumers gain increased control over the quantity and quality of their food access.

This brand of urban locavorism improves resilience in a number of ways. In reducing the physical distance between spaces of production and consumption, dependence on corresponding energy-intensive systems, such as refrigeration, storage, distribution, and transportation, also diminishes. Due to the spatial constraints of cities, urban gardens generally occupy smaller land parcels than their rural counterparts, which in turn reduces a crop's vulnerability to diseases and pests, as well as demands for broad-scale inputs and heavy machinery. Moreover, the independent parcels of land themselves are dispersed and independently managed—individual experiments that Lister calls "safe-to-fail" rather than "fail-safe."[18] Such an extensive infrastructure must necessarily attract substantial citizen participation in order to scale up; in Cuba this movement was adopted by Habaneros simply because it helped them identify their next meal.

Beyond an impressive growing capacity and all-too-incredible production numbers, Havana's urban farming system also fosters social and civic engagement that indicates the development of a higher resilience index.[19] Much as the Country Life Movement signaled a shift in values as well as in actions in the United States, in Cuba the increasing popularity of city farming marks a step forward in the evolution of urban identity.[20] Here, the change in agricultural yields supported socialist ideals broadly and signaled the transformation of society. As a response to real-world needs, Cuba structured viable strategies for social and agricultural change.

This model for post-oil resilience provides a compelling counterpoint to the U.S. food system, in which massive-scale industrial food production supports an illusion of permanent abundance. Its corporate agribusiness relies on a system of heavy inputs and unsound farming practices, including the application of environmentally detrimental pesticides, the widespread use of energy-intensive machines, and the reliance on monoculture crops. The incredible yields that this system generates—which make up approximately 98 percent of the food grown in the United States—rest on the shaky foundation of "mechanically and chemically intensive farming methods for the maximization of profit."[21] As agricultural systems around the world become more heavily taxed, there is good evidence that this U.S. model is not sustainable. To be sure, factors such as climate change, urban development, foreign-oil dependence, and ever-dwindling natural resources threaten to erode this system in the future.[22]

In this sense, food access has resurfaced as a matter of national security for the United States today. Similar to the position in which Cuban citizens found themselves in 1989, Americans are dependent on calories tied to a foreign oil supply and an energy-intensive transportation infrastructure, either of which could collapse at any moment.[23] In both resource-poor and post-crisis scenarios, whether occurring in the United States or elsewhere, food security will track resilience factors, such as diversity, sustainability, and redundancy. Large farms—whose appetite for irrigation, oil, and chemistry, not to mention reliance on economic subsidies—simply cannot offer the resilience of a diverse-but-interconnected system of small farms.

Urban farming reinforces food security in a dispersed and transparent way. While jumping scales from the tiny island nation of Cuba to the vast geography and large consumption demands of the United States appears to be illogical, the two countries share similar cultural, social, technological, and even urban DNA. For instance, much of the common anatomy that fosters productive urban landscapes—the rooftop, the vacant lot, or the pocket park—occurs with similar regularity in each country. While eliminating dependence on foreign oil and food imports appears on the surface to be an audacious demand, the idea of the resurrection of a victory-garden approach seems much more manageable. It is worth remembering, after all, that in 1943 Americans planted more than twenty million victory gardens, and the resulting harvest accounted for nearly one-third of all of the vegetables consumed in the United States that year.[24]

NOTES

1. Charles Waldheim, "Notes Towards a History of Agrarian Urbanism," in *Bracket 1: On Farming* (Barcelona: Actar, 2010), 18.

2. Ibid.

3. Ibid. According to Charles Waldheim, "this renewed interest in the relation of food production to urban form has been made possible by increased public literacy about food and the forms of industrial food production and distribution that characterize globalization."

4. Charles Waldheim, "Urbanism After Form," in *Pamphlet Architecture 30: Coupling: Strategies for Infrastructural Opportunism*, ed. Neeraj Bhatia et al. (New York: Princeton Architectural Press, 2011), 4.

5. Ibid., 4. Waldheim is talking about the *Pamphlet Architecture 30* authors, but is also referring to the broadening of the field of architecture to include urbanists.

6. Nina-Marie Lister, "Sustainable Large Parks: Ecological Design or Designer Ecology," in *Large Parks*, ed. Julia Czerniak and George Hargreaves (New York: Princeton Architectural Press, 2007), 36.

7. Friedman's book, *The World Is Flat*, highlighted the global trend toward interconnected trade, yet Cuba stood out as one of the few countries moving into isolation.

8. Lawrence J. Vale and Thomas J. Campanella, "Introduction: The Cities Rise Again," in *The Resilient City: How Modern Cities Recover from Disaster*, ed. Lawrence J. Vale and Thomas J. Campanella (New York: Oxford University Press, 2005), 7.

9. Jared Diamond, *Collapse: How Societies Choose to Fail or Succeed* (New York: Penguin Books, 2005), 14.

10. Reyner Banham et al., "Non-plan: an experiment in freedom," *New Society*, March 20, 1969, 435-443.

11. Ingo Vetter, "Urban Agriculture," in *Shrinking Cities 1*, ed. Philipp Oswalt (Ostfildern-Ruit [Germany]: Hatje Cantz, 2005), 493.

12. David Harvey, *Rebel Cities: From the Right to the City to the Urban Revolution* (New York: Verso, 2013), 5.

13. Martin Bourque and Peter Rosset, "Lessons of Cuban Resistance," in *Sustainable Agriculture and Resistance: Transforming Food Production in Cuba*, ed. Fernando Funes et al. (Oakland, CA: Food First Books, 2002), xiv.

14. Bill McKibben, "The Cuba Diet: What Will You Be Eating When the Revolution Comes?," in *Harper's Magazine*, April 2005, 62, http://harpers.org/archive/2005/04/the-cuba-diet/.

15. Max Page, "Narratives of Resilience," *The Resilient City*, 90-91. See also Lance Gunderson and C. S. Holling, eds., *Panarchy: Understanding Transformations in Human and Natural Systems* (Washington, DC: Island Press, 2002).

16. Lyanda Lynn Haupt, *Crow Planet: Essential Wisdom from the Urban Wilderness* (New York: Back Bay Books, 2011), 35.

17. Grahame Shane, "The Emergence of Landscape Urbanism," in *The Landscape Urbanism Reader*, ed. Charles Waldheim (New York: Princeton Architectural Press, 2006), 65.

18. Lister, "Sustainable Large Parks," 46.

19. These production numbers are almost unbelievable because they are so positive, and since the Cuban government presents them they are considered somewhat unreliable.

20. At the turn of the twentieth century, the Country Life Movement romanticized rural living and espoused an altruistic community ethos in the United States.

21. Kathryn A. Peters, "Creating a Sustainable Urban Agricultural Revolution," *Journal of Environmental Law and Litigation 25*, no. 1 (Fall 2010), 207.

22. Ibid., 204.

23. Ibid., 230.

24. Laura J. Lawson, *City Bountiful: A Century of Community Gardening in America* (Berkeley: University of California Press, 2005), 2.

Urban Farming in Cuba

THE DISINTEGRATION OF THE SOVIET BLOC IN 1989 CLIPPED Cuba's umbilical cord and the favorable trade relationships that had long nurtured the island. Without this trade partner, Havana's 2.2 million residents lost access to food imports almost overnight, along with many of the resources needed to sustain their regional agricultural efforts. At that time, Habaneros had not yet developed outlets for widespread food production in the city: they lacked experience, supportive infrastructure, and available land with which to experiment. According to some experts, from 1989 until 1992 Cubans were at risk of mass starvation, having lost one-third of their daily calories, which averaged "thirty pounds in the three long years following the collapse of the Soviet Union."[1] This period was accompanied by the suspension of all but the most critical development activities, such as the transformation of the agricultural sector, and the reduction or elimination of nonessential services, such as garbage collection and public transportation.[2] Cuba's acute economic crisis impacted every sector of society, including food production, education, hygiene, and city services.

Like so many other industrialized nations, Cuba's food system had effectively been outsourced. The Cuban government depended on ideologically aligned trading partners for far more than food products—Cuba relied on them for the oil, mechanical parts, fertilizer, and animal feed that had historically facilitated food production. These inputs served as agricultural gatekeepers, without which the country's single-crop, high-input farming system simply fell apart.[3]

To their credit, Cubans overcame this crisis by refocusing their attention on developing a diverse local foodshed and an ethic of self-sufficiency. Cuban agricultural ministers noted an intentional shift in the country's approach to farming at this time, from the classical model of conventional industrialized agriculture to a more sustainable and context-driven alternative model. In an effort to deindustrialize their food and farming system, farmers followed the principles of low-input sustainable agriculture (LISA) promoted by progressive growers in the United States. In this system, farmers replace "dependence on heavy farm machinery and chemical inputs with animal traction, crop and pasture rotations, soil conservation, organic soil amendments, biological pest control, and what Cubans call *biofertilizers* or *biopesticides*—microbial formulations that are nontoxic to humans."[4]

This semiorganic approach also informed early urban agriculture efforts, and thousands of city farmers in

Havana's historic Vedado neighborhood has clear setbacks and a block structure that facilitates urban growing.

Havana began to carve out space for production. By 2002 at least "86,450 acres of urban Cuban land was dedicated to intensive farming, producing more than 3.2 million tons of food," and in Havana alone at least 12 percent of the city was under cultivation by some 22,000 urban and peri-urban producers.[5] A decade after the food crisis struck, officials estimated that more than 50 percent of the perishable produce consumed in Havana was produced within the city limits.[6]

Despite the dire circumstances that led to the food crisis in 1989, few doubted the ability of Habaneros to improvise and cope, particularly as socialism had honed the Cuban practice of *resolver* over many decades.[7] But flourishing was another matter. Cuba not only survived the aftermath of the collapse of the Soviet bloc and two-plus decades of concomitant trade isolation but also witnessed a fundamental shift in favor of a more resilient infrastructure—all while maintaining strong government and intact social services. Cuba stands apart as a leader in self-provisioning: Not only has the country relied on largely sustainable farming methods during the last twenty-five years, but the island has also innovated new agricultural infrastructures in surprising and unparalleled ways.

Although often misunderstood as an impoverished nation, Cuba possesses a rich social system with high physical quality-of-life indicators. While food access currently consists of basic government-supplied food rations and limited market products, the days of hunger and food insecurity are long gone. The literacy rate is close to 100 percent; the constitution guarantees universal health care, education, and housing; and the country officially maintains an enlightened view toward race and class by declaring racial discrimination illegal.[8] Unlike other regional disasters—notably New Orleans's devastation by Hurricane Katrina in 2005 and Haiti's 2009 earthquake—

35

A produce seller prepares his stall for the day.

this crisis befell a nation with an intact city infrastructure, a history of equitable governance, and strong state leadership.

Cuba is credited as the only country in Latin America to have successfully eliminated hunger—for thirty years preceding the Soviet collapse—only to enter one of the most challenging, pervasive, and inescapable periods of hunger in its history.[9] The food crisis had the effect of refocusing Cuba's food system, creating—among other things—a new model for urban agriculture that is de facto organic, minimally disruptive to the environment, and radically inclusive.

History of Urban Farming in Cuba

The end of the Cuban Revolution in 1959 resulted in a new national food-distribution system reliant on international imports as well as rural and peri-urban agricultural production in Cuba. The First Agrarian Reform Law, passed after the close of the revolution, transferred the ownership of large national and foreign-run *latifundios* (large landed estates) to peasant-run *campesinos* (small-scale farms). A decade later, the Second Agrarian Reform Law effectively eliminated large private farms by decreasing the maximum landholding limit to sixty-seven hectares per individual.[10] During these formative post-revolutionary years, the Cuban government incrementally overhauled every aspect of food provisioning, from restructuring state farms to implementing a ration system.

While this single-system approach adequately provided for the country's needs during this time, farming monopolies and increasingly illogical trade agreements also reinforced near-total dependence on state provisioning. From this perspective, Cuba's food instability was fixed as early as 1972, when the country joined the Council for Mutual Economic Assistance (COMECON) and signed trade agreements with countries such as the Soviet Union (exporting citrus and sugar in exchange for cereals and other staples). This vulnerability was twofold: it both limited Cuba's agricultural products to nonessential, single-export foods and it established a dependence on trade relationships for critical goods.

The genesis of the present-day urban farming movement in Havana dates back to 1966, when urban planners developed the Havana Belt, a swath of farmland encircling the city for concentrated fruit tree and dairy production. Over the years many thousands of city-dwellers have volunteered at this peri-urban space to prepare soil, cultivate seedlings, sow, and harvest. This early urban farm—sponsored by the government and still in place today—trained many Habaneros in the business of agriculture. This notable precedent and a vastly urban population notwithstanding, most of the agricultural production in Cuba occurred in the countryside. [11] Moreover, despite the state's widespread agricultural propaganda, urban dwellers largely experienced a social, geographic, and visual disconnect between farm and table.

When the country lost access to the products that supported food production, such as fertilizers, tractors, parts,

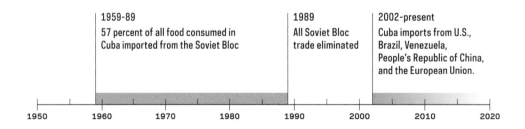

1959-89	1989	2002-present
57 percent of all food consumed in Cuba imported from the Soviet Bloc	All Soviet Bloc trade eliminated	Cuba imports from U.S., Brazil, Venezuela, People's Republic of China, and the European Union.

1950   1960   1970   1980   1990   2000   2010   2020

Cuba's global import relationships over time

and pesticides, with the collapse of the Soviet bloc, it also relinquished the refrigeration, storage, and transportation methods that had sustained Cuba's food distribution system— all of which were dependent upon oil in some way.[12] The government declared the Special Period in Time of Peace in 1991, a wartime-style economic austerity program implemented to ration food as rural farmers struggled to keep up with production demands. Approximately ninety thousand tractors were replaced by two hundred thousand oxen, and the country began "the largest conversion from conventional agriculture to organic or semi-organic farming that the world has ever known."[13]

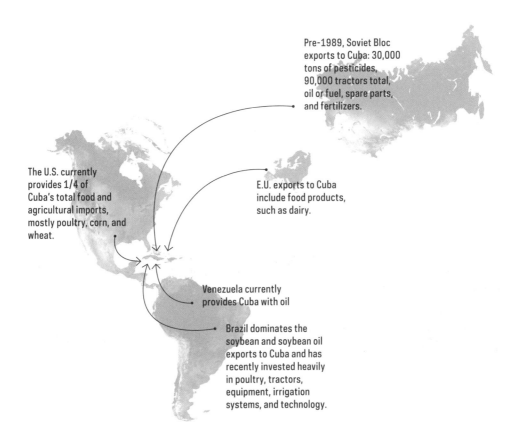

Pre-1989, Soviet Bloc exports to Cuba: 30,000 tons of pesticides, 90,000 tractors total, oil or fuel, spare parts, and fertilizers.

The U.S. currently provides 1/4 of Cuba's total food and agricultural imports, mostly poultry, corn, and wheat.

E.U. exports to Cuba include food products, such as dairy.

Venezuela currently provides Cuba with oil

Brazil dominates the soybean and soybean oil exports to Cuba and has recently invested heavily in poultry, tractors, equipment, irrigation systems, and technology.

The Special Period also contributed to the widespread popularization and prevalence of urban agriculture. For the first time since the revolution, devastating food shortages prompted the government to allow individuals to adopt self-provisioning methods. The state announced that government-owned urban lots would be available for agricultural production, officially launching an era of local and decentralized food production.

This shift also marked a change in the individual's relationship to public space: Habaneros now had an invitation—if not a responsibility—to participate openly in their own hyper-local food production. Urban farming reallocated agricultural responsibilities while simultaneously scaling food production

A team of oxen prepares the soil at an organopónico.

in new ways, turning "everyone's attention to smaller spatial scales, such as the neighborhood, in ways that signaled an important reconfiguration of prior government practices."[14] This public awareness served as a powerful reframing device, especially in cities, where residents were less likely to feel invested in food production, conceive of opportunities for participation, or imagine spatial alternatives to the traditional farm.

The Cuban government's emphasis on urban farming had two important political outcomes: This framework improved food access in urban areas and united citizens around a common productive goal, both of which reduced the likelihood of civic unrest. By 1992 the chronic food crisis had inspired thousands of Habaneros to claim urban spaces for crop and animal production. The government supplied botanical and agamic seeds, necessary tools, and watering cans, and began to invest resources and financing in the development of *organopónicos* within Havana's city limits.[15]

Cuba's food crisis intensified the same year, however, when the U.S. Congress passed the Torricelli Act, banning trade between Cuba and foreign subsidiaries of U.S. companies. Under this new law, boats stopping in Cuban ports would not be permitted to land in the United States for six months, which effectively eliminated trade stopovers in Cuba. This loss of trading partners deepened the island's economic crisis, forcing Cuba to turn inward to solve problems of food provisioning, agricultural training, and pest control.

In 1993 Fidel Castro responded with the Third Agrarian Reform Law, which allowed for the transfer of 70 percent of Cuba's agricultural land—through usufruct rights—to individuals and to peasant associations and cooperatives for farming.[16] This statute had an immense impact on Havana's peri-urban ring, which became an essential production area for farming,

41

due to its proximity to Habaneros's tables. Within a year many
new farmers were growing food, largely without information
or experience but buoyed by the resources provided by the
government. Independent gardens and farms could now be
found in every neighborhood in Havana.

By 1995 food shortages had begun to lessen—a direct
result of the urban farming initiatives in Havana, where scarcity
"was largely overcome through domestic production increases
that came primarily from small farms, and, in the case of
eggs and pork, from booming backyard production."[17] Although
Cuba's food situation had stabilized by the mid-nineties,
the already strained trade relationship with the United States
further declined with the Helms-Burton Act of 1996. This act
tightened trade embargos and worsened the economic situation
for Cubans. Ironically, while the ever-tightening U.S. trade
embargos were meant to overwhelm Cuba, they may have
unexpectedly strengthened the country's self-sufficiency and
reinforced Castro's power.

Many physical and organizational changes impacted
urban farming infrastructure during the nineties, including
the authorization of more than two hundred thousand
self-employment licenses (many in the farming industry);
the transition of more than 2.6 million hectares of state-owned
land given to Basic Units of Cooperative Production (BCUPs) for

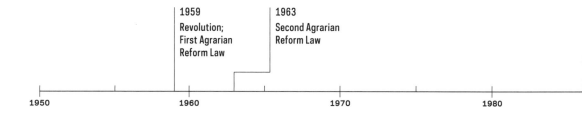

1959
Revolution;
First Agrarian
Reform Law

1963
Second Agrarian
Reform Law

1950   1960   1970   1980

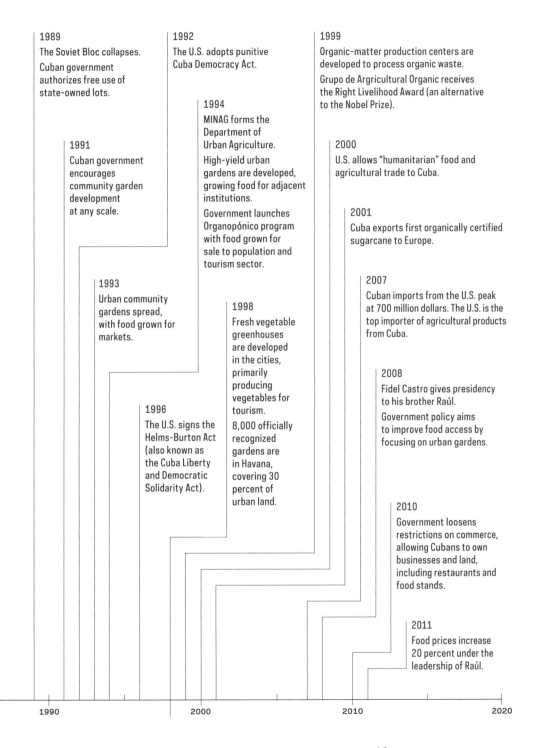

1989
The Soviet Bloc collapses.
Cuban government
authorizes free use of
state-owned lots.

1991
Cuban government
encourages
community garden
development
at any scale.

1993
Urban community
gardens spread,
with food grown for
markets.

1996
The U.S. signs the
Helms-Burton Act
(also known as
the Cuba Liberty
and Democratic
Solidarity Act).

1992
The U.S. adopts punitive
Cuba Democracy Act.

1994
MINAG forms the
Department of
Urban Agriculture.
High-yield urban
gardens are developed,
growing food for adjacent
institutions.
Government launches
Organopónico program
with food grown for
sale to population and
tourism sector.

1998
Fresh vegetable
greenhouses
are developed
in the cities,
primarily
producing
vegetables for
tourism.
8,000 officially
recognized
gardens are
in Havana,
covering 30
percent of
urban land.

1999
Organic-matter production centers are
developed to process organic waste.
Grupo de Argricultural Organic receives
the Right Livelihood Award (an alternative
to the Nobel Prize).

2000
U.S. allows "humanitarian" food and
agricultural trade to Cuba.

2001
Cuba exports first organically certified
sugarcane to Europe.

2007
Cuban imports from the U.S. peak
at 700 million dollars. The U.S. is the
top importer of agricultural products
from Cuba.

2008
Fidel Castro gives presidency
to his brother Raúl.
Government policy aims
to improve food access by
focusing on urban gardens.

2010
Government loosens
restrictions on commerce,
allowing Cubans to own
businesses and land,
including restaurants and
food stands.

2011
Food prices increase
20 percent under the
leadership of Raúl.

1990   2000   2010   2020

farming; and, in 1994, the approval of a new type of agricultural market, with prices responding to supply and demand.[18] Physically, the city of Havana exhibited a host of new spatial outcomes supporting these bourgeoning initiatives, including education and dissemination centers, markets and farm stands, and many scales of urban farms.

In 1997 Fidel Castro approved a new model for profit sharing through the organopónicos, where farmworkers could augment their base salary with earnings from surplus produce. Journalist Damien Cave has since called this permissible form of entrepreneurship "handcuffed capitalism," and many Cubans acknowledge that the market remains heavily restricted by the government.[19] This allowance, however, made farming wildly popular in Cuba,where salaries fixed by the government hover around thirty American dollars a month and it is illegal to engage in most other forms of private entrepreneurship.[20] This model proved to be a tremendous success, as market forces stimulated better crop yields, which in turn bolstered the nation's foodshed.

By 2001 food security was under control in Havana, with a host of urban farming initiatives creatively appliquéd onto the old fabric of the city. Productive urban gardens played an instrumental role in this self-sufficiency, where "the shift to urban agriculture required important revisions to established ways of envisioning both urban and agricultural space, as well as food provisioning, within Socialist Cuba."[21] Urban farming was included in the city's master plan as early as 2000, a decision that served to legitimize this ecology as a fixture of Havana's foodshed.[22]

Current Practices

Havana's urban agriculture experiment can now be called a model, having flourished for more than two decades and produced a host of sophisticated new practices and forms. These innovative urban efforts—combined with the transition to semiorganic farming in rural areas—have established Cuba as a world leader in sustainable food production. In a country where more than 75 percent of the population currently resides in cities and towns, urban agriculture provides an important outlet and service for residents who have been exposed to food insecurity.[23] Over the last decade, Habaneros have generated a number of different farm typologies, in a network of intensive and largely organic farms throughout the city, that collectively produce one hundred thousand tons of vegetables and herbs every year. Moreover, this movement

Repurposed roofing tiles form the edge condition of many raised beds.

45

has also begun to rebuild the economy with a direct rise in jobs: In 1989, there were no documented urban farming workers and within a decade, the number rose to 22,781 agricultural laborers in Havana alone.[24]

The adoption of self-provisioning by Habaneros has also ushered in new attitudes and habits around eating. One of the major changes that emerged from this crisis was a cultural reframing, a reorientation toward dishes that incorporate locally available foods. For instance, *viandas*—the popular roots and tubers that grow easily in the Cuban climate—have become a primary food source, substituting the more elusive wheat, rice, and animal protein that had defined the island's diet.[25] While these eating and cooking habits surfaced as a response to the food crisis, they also mark a return to the sustainable food culture that once characterized the island.

An entire monthly ration for two people, circa 2012

The benefits of urban farming have been well documented. This practice improves food security and access to fresh food, encourages productive use of vacant or underused areas of the city, and promotes a culture of healthy eating. Low-input gardens provide many environmental benefits, from the elimination of informal dumpsites and increase of green spaces to the improvement of animal habitats, water management, and air quality. City gardens reduce the urban heat-island effect, preserve soil health, and create vegetative buffers against hurricanes. The creative reuse of vacant space in the city—combined with the reappropriation of biodegradable waste streams and the

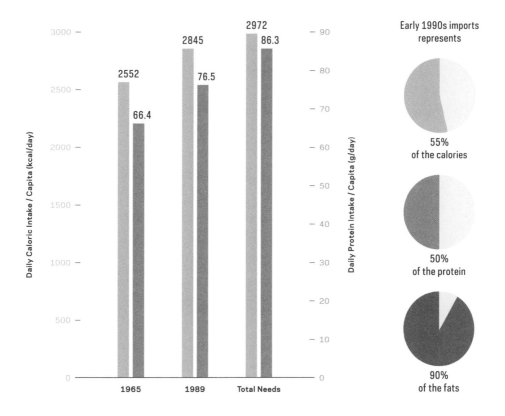

near elimination of energy-intensive transportation—helps to solidify this movement's viability in the face of diminishing resources. In Havana this effort has also spurred an open and collective participation not found in previous modes of rural agricultural practices. Called "civic agriculture" by sociologist Thomas Lyson and "everyday urban agriculture" by educators Michael Nairn and Domenic Vitiello, this brand of urban farming involves diverse participants and stakeholders, strengthens food justice, and has generated many thousands of associated jobs.[26]

Although urban farms offer a host of unique benefits, they reveal additional challenges stemming from their immediate urban context. Environmental pollution and urban toxins from salvaged materials, contaminated soils, and motorized vehicles could seriously compromise the health and viability of food products. Water scarcity remains problematic in Havana, where 38 percent of crop irrigation draws from the public water system, and more than half of the water moving through that network never reaches the spigot.[27] Farmers who do not have long-term land tenure have little incentive to invest in infrastructure, inhibiting planning efforts for a more long-term and resilient system. Critics also note that farms lack integration into the existing urban fabric "not only aesthetically, which no doubt is an important factor in any working environment, but also in relation to other components of the urban environment— be they natural, economic, or social."[28]

Today Cuba enjoys greater food security than ever before but continues to rely on foreign trading partners such as Venezuela, China, Brazil, and the United States for imported food products.[29] Cubans now have access to an appropriate number of recommended daily calories through some combination of the ration system; state, free, and black markets; and self-provisioning. During the first decade of the twenty-first century, many Cubans lacked adequate access to protein; butter, cheese, milk, and meat were all in short supply. Because animals rely on feed—previously imported and currently still difficult to source—their populations have not yet rebounded on the island. While caloric intake meets or exceeds world standards, many Cubans today still struggle to secure a balanced diet that includes all of the relevant food groups.

This food stress stems from a lack of opportunity in a city where, as author Jennifer Cockrall-King reminds us, "between food and clothing expenses, there's little left over for even everyday luxuries."[30] The basic state ration provides only some of the staples that might be required to construct a balanced meal. Additional food, as well as medicine, transportation, entertainment, and material goods must be purchased using the nominal monthly allowance provided by the government. But this resource scarcity and the corresponding economy with which many Cubans organize their lives is one of the reasons that this country appears to have such a strong environmental ethic— in 2006 the World Wildlife Foundation identified Cuba as the only country in the world with sustainable development.[31]

However, conspicuous consumption has soared during the last decade as U.S. embargoes and blockades have loosened, increasing Cuba's connection to the outside world. Despite this rising buying power, many good reasons remain for supporting the urban farming movement in Havana, not the least of which has been the increased control that growers have gained over their own food access. Because the state's highest quality agricultural goods are reserved for the tourist industry and only second-tier produce is available at markets, self-provisioning remains one way for Cubans to transcend limited market options. The number of urban farms—of all types—

49

in Havana has actually increased since 1996, and agricultural yields and popular interest also continue to rise.[32]

During the last two decades, Cuban growers have had the freedom to explore urban farming directly, without typical barriers to entry, such as permitting, fees, or land acquisition. Although the physical form of these urban farms was limited by available building materials, tools, and technologies, these constraints have also encouraged and resulted in responsive designs that adapt according to community needs

A *parcelero* waters the many potted plants on his lot, using water brought to the site and stored in barrels.

and government directives. This organic development has led to flexibility in farm typology and aesthetics, with designs that respond to production, context, and market forces. For better or worse, the development of urban agriculture in Cuba has been characterized by a lack of formal or professional design guidance.

Regardless, Havana's innovative urban agriculture movement has helped to inspire new thinking around planning and design, especially now that the food crisis has been resolved. This is an unusual and unexpected outcome in the context of an architecture and urban planning process that political scientist James Scott attributes to "authoritarian, high-modernist states," which tend to be more interested in prioritizing technology, efficiency, and state control.[33] In adopting urban agriculture initiatives, the Cuban government implicitly condoned small-scale alternatives, both by allowing for the reappropriation of civic landscapes that had previously served other functions and by acknowledging the failure of industrial-scale agriculture. Anthropologist Adriana Premat considers this shift to be fundamental in the evolution of the Cuban state identity, as "the country was 'forced' to move away from previously hegemonic conceptualizations of space, and from forms of food production and distribution that advocated rational, large-scale planning and full integration into the formal state apparatus."[34]

Context and Conditions

While in large part the result of production demands, Havana's urban farming movement has also been shaped by the city's climate, urban form, and socialist ethic. Cuba's tropical climate, with its balmy temperatures and reliable rainfall, allows for year-round cultivation and a wide diversity of crop types.[35] Urban farms host varied and diverse produce, ranging from hardy regional crops well suited to the climate (viandas, plantains, coffee) to nonnative foods acquired through international trade (rice, wheat), which have long been assimilated into the Cuban diet.

More than 75 percent of the Cuban population lives in urban areas, of which Havana is the largest and most populous, with 2,156,650 inhabitants.[36] The formal layout of the city is a dense radial configuration of neighborhoods that developed incrementally over the last five hundred years. Historically, Habaneros relied on harvests from rural areas for food; today, the vast tracts of peri-urban lands that border the city closely resemble rural landscapes and, because they are officially part of Havana, significantly boost the city's productive yields.

Plots of land in the heart of the city also contribute to Havana's production numbers. But unlike the peri-urban landscapes, agricultural sites within Havana's urban core necessarily responded to the primarily extensive development that had already taken place there—most of these plots are entirely made up of leftover waste spaces. With the exception of greenbelt farms and several food parks, Havana's urban farming spaces have not been designed into the urban fabric— so much as seized—according to opportunity and convenience.

Each of Havana's unique neighborhoods conforms to its own specific block and lot structure. Given this strict standard, it is easy to identify correlations between farm type and city form: Smaller garden plots correspond to the dense, central, and oldest parts of the city; medium-sized tracts tend to be located in residential areas just outside of the central core; and the largest growing spaces occur in peri-urban zones. There is also a connection between the type of space and the grower: Smaller farms tend to be single-family ventures, while the government owns larger landholdings (many of which are subsequently borrowed by workers' collectives and farming clubs). In this socialist state, the resources that are available to small-scale growers are limited, as only cooperatives and other large-scale initiatives receive financial support from the government. As a result, much of the physical infrastructure

Map showing the density of gardens in the Vedado.

that supports urban growing—from storage spaces and market stands to fencing and irrigation—occurs at the scale of the larger farm.

Despite widespread support and engagement, Havana's robust farming movement still faces many challenges. The city's crumbling physical infrastructure, frequent electricity brownouts, and vulnerability toward hurricanes and cold fronts impact agricultural yields and the projected continuation of many urban farms. Access to clean and plentiful water for crop irrigation is one of the most persistent obstacles for farmers, and, if not addressed, could effectively cap the number of farms found in Havana. In the case of temporary growing spaces, soil health has not been prioritized over yields, which could lead to the gradual degradation of soil quality.[37] Additionally, concerns about the safety of the soil in urban lots have required growers to use raised beds with imported soils.

Land Use

In the absence of a progressive planning agenda through which agricultural space might be strategically allocated, urban farming initiatives tend to rely on the opportunistic reappropriation of abandoned or underused lands. In densely populated cities across the globe it is often difficult to secure space for cultivation, especially in places where land values have already effectively priced out farming. Environmental activists and urban survivalists consider this land-use disparity to be a particularly fraught issue, as urban gardens that could be used to infuse vitality are routinely displaced by more profitable ventures. In *Resilient Cities*, authors Peter Newman, Timothy Beatley, and Heather Boyer champion the more equitable integration of development and productive spaces from a planning perspective, which they envision as producing food as well as "potential sources of renewable energy, especially the production of biocrops and biofuels."[38]

In the wake of Cuba's food crisis, the government immediately adjusted land-tenure laws to support urban farming endeavors. Socialist theory allows for multiple forms of land tenure, and—according to agricultural ecologist Richard Levins—the Cuban government's "transfer of land management from state farms to cooperatives was no abandonment of socialism but a reorganization within socialism to meet socialist goals better."[39] Naturally, private property presents an obstacle to space appropriation for urban agriculture; in Havana the new regulations only released public (government-owned) spaces for open-access food production. This strategy worked in part because the government still held many acres of public lands in the city, and this land formed Havana's new productive commons: a network of urban farms in parks and public open spaces.

Usufruct rights, which allow individuals to use government lands for their own initiatives, became the legal framework under which Cubans reappropriated land for farming.[40] From the scale of a family garden to the large public food park, usufruct was used to free up land for food production. Vacant lots, public parks, and even median strips—all underproductive landscapes from the government's perspective—became surfaces for informal gardening. Along with an implicit authorization for agricultural transformation, this legal structure also came with a set of rules—from preserving trees to keeping the land in agricultural production—that has kept, and continues to keep, these spaces viable over time to a variety of users.[41]

Although urban farms in Havana rarely change hands or transition to non-agricultural uses, this shift can legally occur when a lot has remained fallow for six months. This ensures that farmers continually produce crops on state-owned lands, permitting other farmers to step in if a space has been abandoned. There is also a precedent for farmers to change product types over time; many farms have transitioned from planting annuals to investing in lower-maintenance crops and outputs, such as biofuels, composting sites, or orchards, over time.[42] Because this informal agricultural land use lacks permanent protection, in the future these productive spaces may be developed or converted into more permanent green space in the form of forests or parks.

In 2012, President Raúl Castro announced another major change in land ownership: Cubans would be allowed to sell their houses for the first time since the revolution. While the idea of a housing market remains a somewhat foreign concept to Cubans—for six decades citizens had legally owned their houses but could not sell them—it promises to have a profound impact on the economic and physical makeup of the country. To date, most of this activity appears to have affected buildings rather than landscapes, although gardens, farms, and empty lots may begin to change hands in the future. One of the most likely reasons that this new market has not impacted urban farming initiatives in Havana is that the majority of farmed land is government owned and therefore not for sale.[43]

NOTES

1. Jennifer Cockrall-King, *Food and the City: Urban Agriculture and the New Food Revolution* (Prometheus Books, 2012), 286.
2. Maria Caridad Cruz and Roberto Sanchez Medina, *Agriculture in the City: A Key to Sustainability in Havana, Cuba* (Kingston, Jamaica: Ian Randle Publishers, 2003), 4.
3. Peter Rosset and Medea Benjamin, eds., *The Greening of the Revolution: Cuba's Experiment with Organic Agriculture* (Melbourne, Australia: Ocean Press, 2002), 3.
4. Ibid., 5.
5. Peters, "Creating A Sustainable Urban Agricultural Revolution," 233; Cruz and Medina, *Agriculture in the City*, 4.
6. Fifty percent is a conservative number. This figure varies widely between sources and has been often quoted at up to 90 percent.
7. *Resolver* is a verb used frequently in Havana, meaning to resolve or fix a problematic situation.
8. See Appendix A for the 2013 ration. According to the 2002 census, literacy rates in Cuba are 99.8 percent. There are more doctors in Cuba per capita than any other country: 70,000 for a population of 11 million. Christopher Beam, "What's With All the Cuban Doctors?" *Slate*, February 1, 2007, http://www.slate.com/articles/news_and_politics/explainer/2007/02/whats_with_all_the_cuban_doctors.html.
9. Rosset and Benjamin, *The Greening of the Revolution*, 24.
10. Ibid.
11. By the late 1980s at least 69 percent of the Cuban population lived in an urban area, and some 2.2 million people resided in the capital city. Ibid., 15.
12. In the late 1980s, Cuba imported 48 percent of its fertilizers and 84 percent of their pesticides. Ibid., 18; In 1988, 57 percent of total food was imported. Catherine Murphy, "Cultivating Havana: Urban Agriculture and Food Security in the Years of Crisis" (Oakland, CA: Food First Institute for Food and Development Policy, 1999), 1. http://library.uniteddiversity.coop/Food/CultivatingHavana-UrbanAgricultureAndFoodSecurity.pdf
13. Adriana Premat, *Sowing Change: The Making of Havana's Urban Agriculture* (Nashville: Vanderbilt University Press, 2012), 17; Rosset and Benjamin, *The Greening of the Revolution*, 5.
14. Premat, *Sowing Change*, 19.
15. Cruz and Medina, *Agriculture in the City*, 24.
16. Hans-Jürgen Burchardt, *La última reforma agrarian del siglo: la agricultural cubana entre el cambio y el estancamiento* (Caracas, Venezuela: Editorial Nueva Sociedad, 2000), 174; See also Rainer Schultz, "Food Sovereignty and Cooperatives in Cuba's Socialism," in *Socialism and Democracy* 26, no. 3 (2012), 128.
17. Bourque and Rosset, "Lessons of Cuban Resistance," xviii.
18. Cruz and Medina, *Agriculture in the City*, 6.
19. Damien Cave, "How Capitalist Are the Cubans?," *New York Times*, December 1, 2012, Sunday Review, SR6, http://www.nytimes.com/2012/12/02/sunday-review/how-capitalist-are-the-cubans.html.
20. In 2011 President Raúl Castro authorized the private ownership of small independent hotels (*casa particulares*) and restaurants, which, along with farming, are the few opportunities Cubans have to make money independently.
21. Premat, *Sowing Change*, 29.
22. The 1984 master plan did not allocate space for farming except for several large farms at the city's perimeter.

23. Mario González Novo et al., *Testimonios: Agricultura Urbana en Ciudad de La Habana* (Havana, Cuba: Asociación Cubana de Técnicos Agrícolas y Forestales, 2008), 21.
24. Ibid., 11.
25. Rosset and Benjamin, *The Greening of the Revolution*, 25.
26. Thomas A. Lyson, *Civic Agriculture: Reconnecting Farm, Food, and Community* (Medford, MA: Tufts University Press, 2004); Dominic Vitiello and Michael Nairn, "Everyday Urban Agriculture: From Community Gardening to Community Food Security," *Harvard Design Magazine* 30, no. 2 (Fall/Winter 2009); Cruz and Medina, *Agriculture in the City*, 24.
27. Cruz and Medina, *Agriculture in the City*, 52, 60.
28. Ibid., 49.
29. Cuba's major agricultural trading partners are Venezuela, Brazil, China, Canada, Spain, and the United States. Common imports include meat and grain, as well as the mechanical parts, oil, fertilizers, and pesticides used for farming.
30. Cockrall-King, *Food and the City*, 289.
31. This study was based on two indexes: human welfare and ecological footprint. Many Cubans associate this environmental ethic with necessity rather than choice. Julia Wright, *Sustainable Agriculture and Food Security in an Era of Oil Scarcity: Lessons from Cuba* (London: Routledge, 2008), 233.
32. Cruz and Medina, *Agriculture in the City*, 27.
33. James C. Scott, *Seeing Like a State: How Certain Schemes to Improve the Human Condition Have Failed* (New Haven: Yale University Press, 1998), 89-90.
34. Premat, *Sowing Change*, 13.
35. Average temperatures in Havana are 25 degrees celsius (77 degrees fahrenheit), with a relative humidity of 79 percent and an average annual rainfall of 1.4 meters (55 inches). González Novo et al., *Testimonios*, 16.
36. Ibid., 15.
37. Cruz and Medina, *Agriculture in the City*, 29.
38. Peter Newman, Timothy Beatley, and Heather Boyer, *Resilient Cities: Responding to Peak Oil and Climate Change* (Washington, DC: Island Press, 2009), 75.
39. Richard Levins, "The Unique Pathway of Cuban Development," in *Sustainable Agriculture and Resistance*, 278.
40. In Cuba the usufruct typically allows individuals to use government land for a ten-year renewable term and cooperatives for a twenty-five-year renewable term. Schultz, "Food Sovereignty and Cooperatives in Cuba's Socialism," 117-38.
41. On these government lands, no trees are to be cut down, and no structures, other than those strictly necessary for workers and production, are to be built. Those structures, when built, must be "rustic and blend with the landscape." Cruz and Medina, *Agriculture in the City*, 26.
42. One of the most interesting precedents for this type of transitioning model is the Parque Nacional in Havana, where some recreational spaces have been transitioned into agricultural space.
43. However, an estimated 85 percent of Habaneros own their houses, which often have associated gardens. These patios could be impacted by a change in ownership.

Urban Emergency: Community Resilience in Cuba and New Orleans

Zachary Lamb

Emergencies modify existing architecture through the adoption of new regulations and technologies in response to cultural norms about risk, but crises produce whole new architectures.
    —Mark Wigley, "Space in Crisis"

In recent years increasingly frequent hurricanes and tropical storms have caused ever-greater damage as they touched down on the coastlines of the United States. As scholars and policy makers look for guidance on how to avoid catastrophic losses, like those that followed Hurricane Katrina, they frequently look to Cuba's emergency-preparedness programs as an example.[1] While these lessons in emergency preparedness will certainly be useful in preserving lives during and after disasters, the recent revolution in Cuba's food system may hold even more valuable insights for how New Orleans and other cities can respond to crises in ways that address their vulnerabilities and increase long-term resilience.

The primary lesson to be learned from Cuba's food revolution is that crises can invite opportunities to build greater resilience through increased self-reliance, development of local solutions, and investment in human capital. In seeking to improve resilience in cities, planners and designers would do well to consider the Cuban agricultural revolution as an

59

inspiration for how communities can develop informal and community-driven mechanisms of resilience.

The Cuban government has been much praised for the capabilities of the nation's emergency-preparedness and -response systems. Through a highly disciplined and regimented program led by the civil defense forces, the government has proven remarkably effective in preparing the population for disasters, minimizing loss of life, and mobilizing resources in the immediate aftermath of highly disruptive events, such as

A house in post-Hurricane Katrina New Orleans

60

hurricanes.[2] In 2001, Hurricane Michelle barreled into the island nation as a fierce Category 4 storm, even more powerful than Katrina, which was a Category 3 storm when it made landfall near New Orleans. While the flooding that followed Katrina caused thirteen hundred deaths in New Orleans alone, Michelle caused only five deaths in all of Cuba.[3]

While there are clearly valuable lessons to be learned from the Cuban emergency-response system's ability to equitably and efficiently prepare for and respond to extreme events, some components of the system rely on a degree of social solidarity and government control that is likely unrealistic in an American context.[4] Even setting aside the differences in culture and government structure, emergency preparation and response is only a small component of building lasting, community-level resilience.

The innovative response to Cuba's food crises of the 1990s presents an especially useful example of community resilience because it arose not out of systematic state planning efforts but from local necessity and investments in human capital. Whereas the country's civil defense and allied institutions have developed a masterful ability to cope with finite natural disasters, the shock to the nation's food system that followed the collapse of the Soviet Union was a true crisis in that it was "a threat to the whole system."[5] The sudden loss of heavily subsidized fuel and food commodities from socialist trading partners led to major food shortages in Cuba. During this period the calorie consumption of the average Cuban declined by more than a third.[6]

This so-called Special Period and the revolution in food production and distribution that followed created a radically new form of resilience that grew out of a crisis response. With the collapse of the existing trade-dependent system,

Cuban society had to reinvent how it fed itself. In the new energy-constrained reality, local production displaced international trade networks, and low-input organic farming methods replaced chemical- and energy-intensive practices. While the national government supported the development of these new food systems through investments in agricultural research, relaxed regulation on agricultural markets, and support for community growing institutions, the movement was largely driven from the community level. The literal hunger of a deprived but highly educated population drove the development of a distributed system of communal urban gardens, or *organopónicos*, that is now the envy of many highly industrialized countries.

The revolution in Cuba's food system, with its locally generated resilience developed out of necessity, human-capital investment, and newfound isolation, stands in stark contrast to the post-Katrina recovery and redevelopment of New Orleans. The Katrina recovery, on the other hand, has seen the expenditure of tremendous resources without substantial improvement in local resilience or decrease in the risk of future disasters. The combination of inadequate infrastructure, generations of risk-blind development patterns, and radical resource inequality among its population made New Orleans uniquely vulnerable and ill prepared for Katrina. The storm itself, the failure of the city's flood-protection infrastructure, and the inadequate emergency response left 80 percent of the city flooded, 70 percent of structures seriously damaged, more than 100,000 people dislocated for extended periods, and 1,300 people dead.[7] In spite of these dire outcomes, the long-term rebuilding process has not yielded a substantial reduction in the city's vulnerability to future disasters.

Though the flooding that followed Katrina was undeniably devastating for New Orleans, massive waves of outside recovery subsidies and an absence of large-scale political leadership have ensured that the storm remained a finite emergency rather than a transformative crisis like that experienced in Cuba during the 1990s. After Katrina, the devastation wrought by the failure of the engineered pump and levee infrastructure and by unwise development patterns provided a unique opportunity to explore ways to realign the development of the city to reduce its future vulnerability.

In the months following the storm, the Urban Land Institute, along with legions of academic and avant-garde designers and

The batture was barely affected by Hurricane Katrina.

planners, presented plans for urban recovery. Many of these early plans suggested shrinking the footprint of the city and realigning urban development patterns to reduce flood risks and to adapt to changing demographics (the city's pre-Katrina population had substantially shrunk from its 1960s peak). The proposals generated by these early radical reenvisioning processes, like the now infamous Green Dot plan, which proposed to "greenspace" several flood-prone neighborhoods, were immediately and vociferously rejected.[8] Though their economic and ecological rationale was clear, such proposals were doomed by opposition from an unlikely coalition of pro-development interests, political leadership blinded by triumphalist reconstruction narratives, and a deeply distrustful population.[9]

Centuries of urban development that disproportionately victimized low-income African American communities in the cause of urban advancement ensured that any conversation about substantially reforming the size or shape of the city would be immediately poisoned with distrust. In their article, "Three Years after Katrina: Lessons for Community Resilience" geographers Craig Colten and Robert Kates and sociologist Shirley Laska argue that "essential to post-disaster resilience is building an ongoing community-wide commitment to respect all segments of the community and be inclusive in decision-making processes and resource allocation. These measures build trust in advance of the next disaster."[10]

Because New Orleans lacked that essential groundwork of trust between government and broad sections of the population, it was all but impossible to conduct the difficult but essential discussions about reducing the city's vulnerability. This distrust, aligned with the profit motives of construction and real estate interests, led the city to focus on increasing the size and strength of its flood-control infrastructure (pumps, levees, and flood walls), making use of federal funds to redevelop even the most vulnerable, far-flung, and depopulated areas. Rather than reducing vulnerability, this reinvestment in existing infrastructure and risky urbanization patterns reduce the frequency of disruptions from floods, but dramatically increase their severe effects on new developments when they inevitably occur, thus resulting in what has become known as the "levee effect."[11]

Just as the vulnerability of Cuba's food and agricultural policies were laid bare by the collapse of the Soviet system, the catastrophic failure of New Orleans's flood-control systems exposed the inherent risks of relying on highly engineered systems to safeguard the city. While isolation and poverty drove Cuba to develop a more resilient and self-reliant food system in the wake of their crisis, New Orleans's economic and political connections to the larger federal government have allowed the city to resist such a radical adjustment. Thus, in looking for solutions to increased vulnerability caused by the levee effect, it may be most instructive to look outside the levees themselves.

On the outskirts of New Orleans, there is a linear settlement of largely self-built structures tucked incongruously into the willows between the "wrong side" of the levee and the roiling brown water of the Mississippi. This enclave of a dozen dwellings—the last vestige of what was once a settlement of hundreds—is called the *batture*. The buildings and the community of the batture exist largely in spite of the efforts of planning and design professionals, and dominant regulatory and economic structures. Nonetheless, just as Cuba's relocalized food revolution has much to teach about developing resilient local-food systems, there is a tremendous amount to be learned from the batture—and other informal settlements like it—about how cities, buildings, and communities respond to environmental and political vulnerability.

Like Cuba's food-production and -distribution system, the batture can be seen as an example of what urban anthropologist James Holston calls "insurgent citizenship," in which subcommunities carve out new civic spaces for themselves in opposition to, or apart from, dominant, state-defined modes of citizenship. [12] The batture stands in stark contrast to the relatively conventional urban form and culture on the other side of the levee by inverting the bedrock assumptions of risk, infrastructure, and state-dependence that make life at the mouth of the great river possible.

The riverside community's unique forms of adaptation and resilience were on dramatic display in the weeks following

Hurricane Katrina raised many questions of infrastructural stability and resilience.

Katrina. When New Orleans's flood-control systems failed, the batture was largely unaffected. Batture dwellers—living as they do outside of the city's physical and institutional fortifications—do not have the luxury of forgetting their vulnerability and thus have built a community that is armed to respond to environmental threats. Just as Cuba's agricultural revolution emerged in response to newly revealed vulnerability after the fall of the Soviet Union, the batture represents a kind of delta urbanism "without a net," in which residents live without the guarantees of government rebuilding assistance or subsidized flood insurance.

While planner Larry Vale and urbanist Thomas Campanella argue that "resilience is underwritten by outsiders," the post-Katrina recovery of New Orleans and the case of Cuba's food-system revolution present important counterexamples to this "axiom of resilience."[13] In the case of the Katrina recovery, short-term recovery processes underwritten by the federal taxpayers may, in fact, undermine the long-term resilience of the housing and urban development of the city by allocating resources into increasingly hardened infrastructure rather than the reforming of unsound development practices. In contrast, the revolution in Cuba's food system toward greater self-sufficiency and resilience points toward a different model in which relocalization and community solidarity are driven by isolation rather than interdependence.[14]

In the case of post-Katrina New Orleans, the emergency facing the city was severe, but, relative to the geographic expanse and economic resources of the nation as a whole, it was never truly a "threat to the whole system."[15] As such, though the recovery has generated advances in social innovation and increased the capacity of many community institutions, it has not yielded the wholly transformative pivot toward a more resilient and less vulnerable city that many had hoped for. While New Orleans, and the United States, could learn significant lessons from Cuba's emergency-preparation and -response programs, the examples of Cuba's food revolution and the development and evolution of informal communities such as the batture could provide insights into more lasting impact in developing greater urban resilience.

These types of processes create unique mechanisms of resilience because they develop outside of the institutional and infrastructural risk-management regimes of globalized modern life. As such, they may approximate a post-crisis future in which the complex systems underlying the global economy and conventional urban development can no longer be relied upon. In the coming years, the development of more nuanced understanding of how such systems change in response to crisis and vulnerability may allow for innovations that will help to make cities and institutions that are more resilient and better adapted to their environments.

NOTES

1. Martha Thompson and Izaskun Gaviria, *Cuba. Weathering the Storm: Lessons in Risk Reduction from Cuba* (Boston: Oxfam America, 2004).

2. Ibid., 4.

3. Ibid., 9.

4. Ibid., 7.

5. Mark Wigley, "Space in Crisis," *Volume: Bootleg Edition Urban China* (2009): http://c-lab.columbia.edu/0158.html

6. McKibben, "The Cuba Diet," 62.

7. Craig E. Colten, Robert W. Kates, and Shirley B. Laska, "Three Years after Katrina: Lessons for Community Resilience," *Environment: Science and Policy for Sustainable Development* 50 (2008): 36.

8. Yates McKee, "Haunted Housing: Eco-Vanguardism, Eviction, and the Biopolitics of Sustainability in New Orleans," *Grey Room* 30 (2008): 97.

9. Vale and Campanella, "Conclusions: Axioms of Resilience," 339.

10. Colten et al., "Three Years after Katrina," 39.

11. Robert W. Kates, Craig E. Colten, Shirley B. Laska, and S. P. Leatherman, "Reconstruction of New Orleans after Hurricane Katrina: A Research Perspective," *Proceedings of the National Academy of Sciences* 103 (2006): 14653.

12. James Holston, "Spaces of Insurgent Citizenship," in *Cities and Citizenship*, ed. James Holston (Durham and London: Duke University Press, 1999), 157.

13. Vale and Campanella, "Conclusions: Axioms of Resilience," 342.

14. Ibid.

15. Wigley, "Space in Crisis."

Networks and Garden Typologies

Chapter 2

HAVANA'S GROWERS NOW INTERFACE WITH AN INTERCONNECTED-
but-flexible state-supported agricultural network far more
nuanced than the city's previous agricultural infrastructures.
This system is understood as a collection of agricultural-
production typologies ranging in size and type of ownership and
connecting to an equally diverse arrangement of markets and
support services. In relation to the systems of previous decades,
this network offers a more balanced approach to participation
and control: Providers and officials have decentralized the
business of agriculture just enough to maintain flexibility in the
system while retaining enough structure to organize and regulate
this process.

Regardless of farm type, all of the growing efforts in
Havana stand apart from the large-scale rural *fincas* (farms).
The collective operation of many tiny gardens and farms allows
for improved food security over these fincas, both through the
dispersion of resources and from the hands-on investment
of many independent growers. When operating at the intimate
scale of the house or lot, gardens necessarily respond to the
unique context-specific demands of each site. In contrast to Green
Revolution agriculture, which promises efficiency through super-
sized farms, small-but-interconnected urban gardens stand at the
forefront of Cuba's agricultural recovery.[1] Havana may not have
been the first community to shift back to local food production—
many towns have transitioned from industry to agriculture in post-
crisis environments—but it was the first to employ this method
of production comprehensively and across an urban landscape
much like other modern metropolises of the developed world.[2]

Almost all of these gardens utilize land that would otherwise
have been abandoned or left fallow. Landscape architect and
educator Alan Berger calls the creative capitalization of this

drosscape "the great design challenge of the future," and in most cities, the adaptive reuse of these waste landscapes provides an economical and predominately risk-free growing space.[3] Havana's urban gardens typically feature a variety of produce (and occasionally livestock), selected to satisfy the cultural and caloric demands of city dwellers. Products from these gardens supplement the state-sponsored food ration, which does not include fresh vegetables or fruit.

In response to the recent profusion of farming efforts in Havana, there has been an attendant evolution of city form, revealing a host of new agricultural interventions at different scales. Havana's productive spaces range from small backyard

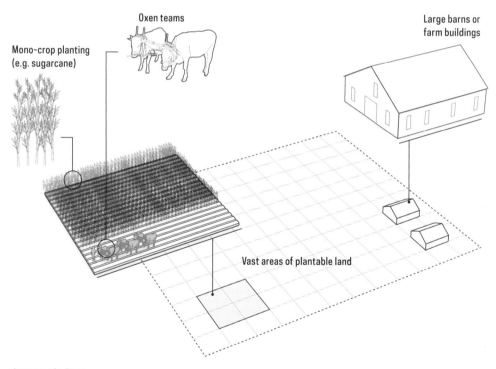

Mono-crop planting
(e.g. sugarcane)

Oxen teams

Large barns or
farm buildings

Vast areas of plantable land

Anatomy of a finca

plots to institutional programs, and include workplace gardens, state-owned farms, and small cooperatives.[4] These landscapes share many similarities across multiple scales, including produce, infrastructure, and farming methods. While the heterogeneity of each plot ultimately stems from site constraints and a grower's needs, most urban farms fall into one of the following four groups: *huertos populares* (popular gardens), *autoconsumos* (institutional gardens), *organopónicos* (cooperative gardens), and *empresas estatales* (state enterprises). Crops include, among others, fresh vegetables and herbs, medicinal and ornamental plants, flowers, fruit, plantains, coffee, cocoa, roots and tubers, oilseeds, rice, beans, corn, and sorghum. Livestock supported by this network includes poultry, rabbits, guinea pigs, sheep, goats, pigs, and cows. Aquaculture and apiaries can be found in far fewer numbers inside city limits.

Cuba's progressive urban agriculture approach stems from a variety of other nonphysical factors as well. These include broad government support in the form of agrotechnology, economic incentives, land tenure and use, social programs, research, and education. Seed banks, markets, and other state organizations provide the support infrastructure for urban agriculture in Havana. These initiatives allow for improved access to farming and gardening as well as the sharing of resources, information, and physical space between growers, and reflect the strong partnership between state-sponsored support and community-engaged activism that many people believe has been essential to Havana's provisioning success. A decentralized distribution network in Havana includes direct sales on farms; state agricultural markets; free markets; agricultural contracts with child-care centers, schools, hospitals and other social programs; and sales to the tourism industry.[5] Technical farming assistance provided by the government is available at agricultural stores, veterinary clinics, compost centers, artisanal pest control centers, seed houses, state-sponsored workshops, and through the many formal and informal gardening clubs in Havana.

Sustainable Urban Farms

One of the most universal responses to food and fuel shortages among Habanero growers has been to prioritize low-input, organic, or permaculture techniques at almost every scale of farm. Researcher Julia Wright suggests that these urban farmers tend to adopt organic methods more successfully than their rural counterparts primarily because they have not been trained to rely on nonorganic methods, while farmer and educator

Intercropping occurs within beds on many small-scale farms.

Fernando Funes attributes Cuba's integrated agroecological platform largely to "the prohibition of chemicals because of proximity to dense human populations."[6] While both of these arguments are valid, it is likely that organic farming in Havana remains popular because pesticides are very difficult to source.

Other examples of sustainable agricultural practices include permaculture methods and advanced low-input growing techniques. Intercropping—growing more than one type of plant in the same space—is a standard practice at all scales of urban farming. Common pairings are plantains and cassava, coffee and taro, corn and taro, and corn and cassava. Waste recycling, in which farms incorporate useful by-products from animals, municipal garbage, green manure, and sugarcane processing is made into compost and is sold throughout the city. Urban farming efforts amplify green spaces in the city, reduce the urban heat-island effect, increase animal habitats, and cleanse both the air and water. Compared to rural fincas, small-scale urban farming causes less ecological disruption and—while increasing overall labor needs—creates valuable jobs.

Although growers and buyers recognize the positive environmental impacts of urban farming, many Habaneros also worry about the lack of environmental testing and regulation in the city. Water and soil testing is not yet common, even in urbanized areas where there are likely pollutants that would affect growing areas. Questionable city-farming practices—such as the use of toxic, salvaged building materials for raised beds in organopónicos or the proximity of vehicular emissions to roadside farms—raise some alarm. Urban gardens are frequently built on contaminated soil or along polluted waterways without monitoring them for safe practices. This relationship with pollution could lead to associated health and environmental impacts and also taint the image of agriculture in the city.

Despite these concerns, Havana's farming system highlights the flexible forms that organically evolve from real-world needs. This growing network provides a road map for a city striving to be independent from oil, inspiring new ways to think about the productive potential inherent in landscapes. As urban designers and architects Mason White, Lola Sheppard, Neeraj Bhatia, and Maya Przybylski suggest, the question of "how to position new infrastructures that confront urgent issues of climate change, sustenance inequality, and environmental degradation" will be the subject of future urban design efforts, and Havana's food system provides a useful template.[7] In building upon this precedent, designers also have the potential to improve their engagement with the environment, using formal and physical constraints as opportunities for innovation.

Farm Types
Spanish Name: *Micro-jardines* (See pp. 92-93.)
English Name: Micro-gardens
Size: Typically less than 100 sq. m.
Date started: Pre-1989
Number: This type of informal gardening is ubiquitous in Havana but not officially recognized or monitored by the state.
Products: Spatially-efficient crops and herbs or small livestock, such as rabbits, guinea pigs, and poultry
Purpose: Self-provisioning
Elements: Small containers, cages, and shading devices
Farmers: Individual home owners or renters
Details: Micro-jardines include planter boxes and potted gardens—the smallest-size garden types in Havana—which are found predominately in the dense central core, where an individual's access to outdoor space is limited. This type of garden is typically privately owned and worked

by one person, for his or her own immediate consumption. Plastic or metal bins hold the growing medium and gardens are often made up of repurposed containers placed on racks, rooftops, or concrete surfaces. Some public-space appropriation occurs at this scale—most often between the sidewalk and the street, where fruit and nut trees or small plants, such as herbs, are grown.

Productive rooftops are a variety of sizes, but are commonly called micro-gardens. They can be found throughout most neighborhoods in Havana and typically incorporate some sort of built-in shading device. Gardeners employ barrels or other container gardens, as well as hutches for livestock. At a spatial level, rooftops represent a protected territory—as much because of their inaccessibility from the street as for their lack of visibility. While the stealing of produce is uncommon in Havana, the separation protects crops from urban scavengers and also simultaneously shields illicit goods from view, such as pigs, which are prohibited in the city center due to sanitary reasons.

Also above street level, cultivated window gardens and balconies typically support small-scale, dense, and valuable crops, making efficient use of space. A 2000 study on urban agriculture noted that urban planners recommend these tiny spaces for the cultivation of medicinal plants, aromatic herbs, and cooking herbs.[8] In the heavily hardscaped central core of Havana, micro-farming efforts help to bring both food and habitat into an otherwise unproductive hardscape.

Spanish Name: *Patios* (See pp. 94–95.)
English Name: Yards
Size: Typically less than 1,000 sq. m.
Date started: Officially monitored by the state in 1991

Number: Informal, ubiquitous, and not always formally registered with the state

Products: Tubers and viandas, vegetables, grain, fruits, small livestock, such as rabbits, sheep, goats, and poultry

Purpose: Self-provisioning

Elements: Containers and bins, cages, perimeter fences, and a compost pile

Farmers: Individual home owners

Details: These small growing spaces are connected to residences, typically worked by one person or a family for private consumption. Approximately 75 percent of residences in Havana are privately owned, and these yards are usually tended by their owners.

Often occurring at a small scale, these gardens fit into underused or leftover spaces within yards and can be easily managed by an individual. The home owner grows items that are particularly suited to existing site conditions, such as soil type or solar access. The close proximity of patios to those who tend them shortens the distance between farm and table and also eliminates the need for commuting laborers.

Spanish Name: *Parcelas* (See pp. 96–97.)

English Name: Lots

Size: Typically less than 1,000 sq. m.

Date started: 1991

Number: 7,944 registered plots in 2000, covering 1,030 hectares (ha) of the city and involving 16,869 farmers

Products: Tubers and viandas, vegetables, grain, fruits, herbs, small livestock, such as rabbits, sheep, goats, and poultry

Purpose: Self-provisioning and small-scale sales or trade

Elements: Perimeter fences, greenhouses, planting beds, occasionally a small stand for street sales

Farmers: Individuals or small groups, usually living nearby

Details: Parcelas are built on usufruct land provided by the government, and could include playing fields, portions of public parks, and abandoned lots, but are generally small- to medium-scale gardens carved out of underused urban areas. They are usually worked by an individual or small group of growers, who produce for their own immediate consumption. Surplus produce can be sold or traded directly from the site. The shape and size ranges from the very private adjacent lot—indistinguishable from a yard—to a much more public and visible urban garden.

Because land—if used for farming—is free in Cuba, urban farming offers individuals with an opportunity to increase their spatial allotment. Parcelas function as an extension of one's residence in that they also often support nonagricultural uses, such as laundry, storage, meditation, and even socializing. However, unlike patios, these areas are understood as communal and recognized as intended for the good of the entire state. Ultimately, parcelas are state owned; thus this land can be revoked if allowed to lay fallow for more than six months. Because parcelas are located on appropriated state lands, their tenure is inherently unstable. Many *parceleros* (small-lot farmers) seek security for this investment by linking to the community in some way—providing food for institutions or inviting school groups on educational tours—to increase their chances at permanency.[9] Indeed, numerous farmers have opened up their space to share with others or to started partnerships with nearby schools, which has helped them to lobby for preservation when developments threaten the sites.

In addition to patios, these huertos populares make up the small-scale self-provisioning lots that are the most common form of urban farming in Cuba today. Havana had approximately one hundred thousand of these in 2002, primarily on vacant lots and backyards. [10] Because these gardens are small enough to be cultivated by an individual—although he or she would need to have an alternative primary source of income—and provide access to diverse, affordable fresh foods, they are extremely common and valued by growers.

These gardens are ubiquitous and widely incorporated into the urban fabric of the city, and they have also been front and center politically as important models for the movement. Premat refers to parcelas as the "inspiring face of Havana's urban agriculture movement." [11] While these gardens are ultimately sanctioned by the state, they appear to be privately owned, both in physical form and management structure, and parceleros benefit from the social status these gardens convey. This perceived sovereignty and small scale helps gardeners to take greater control, as they have more autonomy in the form, production, and oversight of these spaces.

Spanish Name: *Huertos Intensivos* (See pp. 98-99.)
English Name: Intensive Cultivation Gardens
Size: 1,000-5,000 sq. m.
Date started: 1991
Number: 221 in 2000, on 87.26 ha with 663 producers
Products: Primarily fresh vegetables
Purpose: Collective gardening for consumption or trade
Elements: Raised beds; rustic, recycled materials for container beds (stones, roof tiles, pieces of wood); soil brought in from other areas; a retail space for selling to the public
Farmers: Collective growing groups
Details: Larger than parcelas but often still operated as independent businesses, huertos intensivos are single lots under cultivation by private collectives of growers. These medium-sized farms are located throughout the city, often occupying state-owned

land that was once vacant, a field behind a public building, or a piece of a public park. These farms typically are large enough to require multiple employees and can sustain those employees and their families with their produce and profits. Many of these farms specialize in just a few different vegetables or products. After donating a portion of the yields to the state as a tax, the farmers then can legally sell their produce at markets for profit.

Spanish Name: *Autoconsumos* (See pp. 100–1.)
English Name: Self-provisioning Gardens
Size: 1,000–5,000 sq. m.
Date started: 1991
Number: More than 350 in Havana in 2002.
Products: Vegetables and fruits
Purpose: Self-provisioning gardens for schools, workplaces, and factories
Elements: Dependent upon the location and site constraints, as they are attached to institutions; usually raised beds, perimeter fences, and sometimes an orchard
Farmers: Either a dedicated employee or group of employees who share the work of maintaining the garden
Details: Autoconsumos are gardens physically connected to a school or a workplace and are farmed by their employees to support the needs of the cafeteria at that institution. These gardens augment the lunch food that the government provides at each institution, while ensuring that fresh produce will be incorporated into these meals. These gardens represent the efforts of each institution to support socialist ideals by being productive and self-sufficient at multiple scales. Because autoconsumos are hosted by state-run organizations, these growing areas represent solidarity with the country's dispersed and prolific food-security scheme.

Individual autoconsumos are generally started by an
employee within the institution, who works with a larger state-
supported program for these types of gardens. This decision
to farm reflects the physical conditions of the site, such as
presence of growing space, the abilities of the workers, and the
provisioning needs of that population.

Spanish Name: *Organopónico de Alto Rendimiento* (OARS),
or organopónicos (See pp. 102-3.)
English Name: High-yield Urban Gardens
Size: 2,500-20,000 sq. m.
Date started: As early as 1987, but common after 1994
Number: 20 OARS in 2000, on 19.1 ha with 340 producers
Products: Vegetables, especially leafy greens, cooking
herbs and spices, eggs, and fruits
Purpose: Sale to the public and the tourism industry
Elements: Container beds for planting, farming structures
(such as pens for animals), tables and structures for farmers to
use for meals, storage, and meetings, lockable storage areas, a
market stand for selling to the public, and occasionally orchards
Farmers: Work centers or cooperatives pay a fixed salary,
as well as bonuses from profits to these professional growers.
Details: OARS, or state-sponsored farms in Havana,
characterize the most common large-scale farming efforts
within the city's limits. These farms are usually found on infill
sites near housing developments and can stretch across entire
city blocks. Due to their size, these farms tend to be located
on the outer edge of the city, where lower-density development
and block structures afford access to large parcels of land.
Organopónicos usually have long, linear vegetable
beds that are raised six inches above the ground and are bounded
by ceramic roofing tiles. Intercropping and crop rotation are

incorporated to produce high yields with minimal inputs. Often these farms have small outbuildings, such as greenhouses and toolsheds, as well as dedicated non-vegetable production zones for orchards, compost creation, seedlings, herbs, and livestock.

They typically employ several dozen workers who have the opportunity to supplement their monthly salary through profit-sharing. Organopónicos often have signboards and sales tables on site, where workers can monitor real-time revenues from month to month. Organopónicos became Castro's signature gardens as symbolic models for self-sufficiency under socialism, and continue to be revered by both the state and Habaneros today.

Spanish Name: *Campesinos Particulares* (See pp. 104–5.)
English Name: Private Peasant Gardens
Size: 5,000–80,000 sq. m. per farm
Date started: Pre-1989
Number: 2,200 small farms inside city limits in 1999
Products: Soil compost, tree and plant nurseries, flowers, animals, viandas, vegetables, grains, herbs, honey, and fruits
Purpose: Sale to the public, tourists, and public and state agencies; some farms donate to day care and primary schools
Elements: Mounded rows for planting and occasionally orchards, farming structures, market stand, storage sheds for equipment, farmers' residences, windmills, and irrigation systems
Farmers: Individual farmers and their families, or collectives
Details: Located primarily in the green belt or peri-urban Havana, these farms are a part of the urban campesino. One important case study is the *Parque Metropolitano de la Habana* project, a 700-hectare food park within city limits. Conceived as a green lung for the city, the park contains a zoo, a botanical garden, a section of the Almendares River, and numerous recreation areas. There have been farms—as well as orchards—in this park since

the eighteenth century, primarily tended by the Chinese emigrant community. In the early 1990s, as a result of the food stress during the Special Period, farmers joined together to form an agricultural collective with the goal to make their production processes urban, agroecological, intensive, and sustainable.[12] The 96 growers working in the Parque cultivate 78.5 hectares of land, which includes a cooperative, small lots used by individual producers, and an agriculture and forestry unit. The salaried workers and the growers living in the area—who have historically farmed this land—also continue to cultivate their original land.

Spanish Name: *Empresas Estatales* (See pp. 106–7.)
English Name: State Enterprises
Size: 5,000 sq. m.
Date started: Pre-1989
Number: N/A
Purpose: These farms produce food for the state ration, the free market, and the state-controlled tourism sector.
Elements: Greenhouses, fields, fruit plantations (such as orchards), animals, buildings, and terraces for water management.
Farmers: Groups of farmers, working for the state
Products: Vegetables, herbs, eggs, fruits, and meat production. Orchards include varieties of banana, coffee, mango, coconut, avocado, and trees for both wood and shade.
Details: Empresas Estatales are businesses owned by the state and there are two types in Havana: one deals in livestock and the other in orchards for vegetables and fruits. Located at the peri-urban edge of Havana, these large farms occupy a single uninterrupted footprint and tend to isolate crop types into discrete areas. These state-run farms use a combination of oxen teams and tractors, and organic growing methods and pesticides.

Spanish Name: *Mataderos* (See pp. 108-9.)

English Name: Animal Husbandry

Size: 100 sq. m. and more

Date started: Pre-1989

Number: N/A

Products: Meat, such as chickens, ducks, goats, pigs, rabbits, and guinea pigs, and their by-products

Purpose: To provide urban space for formal, hygienic, and regulated animal husbandry

Elements: Cages or pens, feed, shading devices, and water

Farmers: Individuals or small groups

Details: Animals are seamlessly woven into the urban fabric of Havana. Chickens walk freely on the streets or roost in trees, and it is not uncommon to see goats hobbled in public parks or along median strips. These animals are sold to restaurants and markets directly, or are eaten by owners. However, these informal efforts occasionally spread disease of contribute to neighborhood conflict.

In an effort to facilitate this independent animal husbandry, a livestock-advocacy group (ACPA) supports farmers in the city by helping individuals manage flocks and larger animals, providing pens and supplies, and employing a team of veterinarians for house calls. ACPA serves as an intermediary between growers and the state, helping to communicate new government directives, monitoring trends, and aggregating data through 100 service centers, 21 training classrooms, and 16 centers for improving animals. The rules governing these animals have changed regularly, and in some urban areas, particularly downtown Havana, many animals are restricted. Many urban farmers have had to quickly slaughter or "find new homes" for their animals when the laws shifted, especially if a public official was to visit the farm. Chickens, pigs, and rabbits have all been alternately permitted and prohibited since 1989, depending on the year and neighborhood.

Unlike other farm types, animal husbandry presents one form of urban agriculture that involves discretion in Cuba. Many livestock owners keep secret pens for animals and rely on their neighbors to turn a blind eye. This issue underscores the importance of government support in farming measures and points to the still-unresolved access to protein for many citizens.

Livestock Types:

Guinea pigs: These have been called the perfect animal in Havana—easy to care for, safe, and well suited to urban environments. The Ministry of Agriculture (MINAG) made a major campaign to increase their numbers in the early 2000s.[13]

Rabbits: Many people—sometimes in partnership with informal groups—raise or breed rabbits for food. Rabbit meat can be sold dressed directly to individuals or restaurants.

Pigs: An African swine fever epidemic broke out in Havana in 1971, and the government proceeded to restrict pig rearing in the Havana province until 1990. According to permaculture activist Maria Caridad Cruz, unauthorized small-scale pig production was found in even the most urban parts of the city, including inside buildings and houses in the 1990s.[14] Today these urban pigs have been gradually eliminated due to health risks and government regulations, but some illicit operations can still be found in Havana's gardens and front yards. In 1994, collective pig-raising spaces were established by government agricultural agencies as a means of improving city sanitation. These areas are generally located in peri-urban zones—typically three kilometers from urban development and one kilometer from water-supply sources—and are overseen by the state-sponsored Veterinary Medicines Directorate. In 2002, after the end of the worst of the food crisis and in an effort to improve city sanitation,

Fidel Castro launched an official campaign to end pig rearing in the city.[15] However, many urban growers have continued to raise pigs in secret.

Poultry: In the first decade of the food crisis, the government provided urban dwellers with baby chicks to rear in their homes, as a response to chicken and egg shortages.[16] This was a form of micro-husbandry that took advantage of household waste, as one chicken could arguably live off of the food waste produced by a single household. Ducks and turkeys are also common in the city, and all of these birds can be found either contained or roaming freely throughout Havana.

Goats: Often hobbled in public areas for grazing, goats are kept for milk, meat, and carrying goods.

Cows: Cows are not permitted inside the city proper, but they can be found in the Havana Belt and at several state-sponsored organopónicos. Because milk is not widely available in Cuba, self-provisioning through small-scale cow shares is a possibility in the future.

Bees: Honeybees have largely been relegated outside the city limits, due to fear of stings, although non-stinging varieties exist within city limits. Honey is less useful to Cubans, due to each person's ample sugar ration. While not difficult to source, honey could be viewed as a luxury item in Havana. It is sold on the free market, and specialty restaurants sell honey-sweetened mojitos at twice the price of a cane sugar version.

Aquaculture: The Aquaculture Development Program of Havana was launched in 1994 and has a modest number of holdings with small reservoirs for raising freshwater fish. Individual farmers may also have fish in their patios or parcelas.

Spanish Name: *Invernaderos* (See p. 110.)
English Name: Fresh Vegetable Greenhouses

Size: 500–1,000 sq. m.

Date started: 1998

Number: 70 in Havana, located in the *Empresa de Cultivos Varios* and in Free Zones

Products: Primarily vegetables, which need protection from the elements and pests, tomatoes, and seedlings

Purpose: Primarily to sell to the tourism sector but also freely in the state's convertible currency. Products that do not meet tourist standards are sold at a much lower price to locals.

Elements: Insect screens, greenhouse structures, and growing medium in trays

Farmers: *Unidades Básicas de Producción Cooperativa* (UBPC, or Basic Units for Cooperation) workers

Details: These greenhouses moderate sun, wind, and rain exposure to provide a semi-protected growing space. These structures provide local climate control, an extension of the growing season, more effective irrigation for crops, and consistent, year-round jobs. They are staffed by farmers who often also tend open fields, and thus are generally located adjacent to these larger growing spaces. Some greenhouses have double-walled doors and windows for additional protection, and many of these structures limit access by farmers in an effort to reduce contamination.

Spanish Name: *Tiendas Consultorios Agropecuario* (TCAS) (See p. 111.)

English Name: Agricultural Support Stores

Size: N/A

Date started: 1991

Number: 52 TCAS, at least 1 per municipality in Havana

Products: Seeds, seedlings, books and resources, organic compost, veterinary medicine, tools, and ornamental plants

Purpose: Disseminating information and providing assistance to both established and new farmers, addressing questions related to both agriculture and animal husbandry

Elements: Each of the stores is almost identical, made up of the same core elements. They consist of a small, fenced outdoor space for plants, and a lockable shipping container with an operable shutter, signage, and a counter.

Farmers: Each TCA is staffed by one or two agricultural experts employed by the state.

Details: TCAS are located in every neighborhood, and usually have seeds, tools, and a resident farming expert, engineer, or technician on staff—paid by commission—to answer questions and provide training. Serving to educate and support, TCAS function as seed and seedling exchanges, as well as hubs for information, free meetings, and workshops. The TCAS physical building (which is typically a retrofitted shipping container) has a small footprint and is surrounded by a cleared surface for plants. TCAS are open to the public and operate during normal business hours.

Spanish Name: *Las Casas de Posturas* (See p. 112.)

English Name: Seedling Greenhouses

Size: 2,500 sq. m.

Date started: 1996

Number: 11 in 8 municipalities generally found in suburban locations. The greenhouse covers roughly 50 percent of each site.

Products: Seedlings for sale to other programs within the agricultural support network

Purpose: To provide seedlings to TCAS, individual farmers, and cooperatives

Elements: Insect screens, soils from organic-matter production centers, trays for seedlings, and a drip-irrigation system

Farmers: UBPC workers

Details: Las Casas de Posturas ensure that many plants can be disseminated throughout the city and provide high-quality seedlings for the various types of agriculture in Havana. The structures incorporate solar energy (rather than grow lights) through passive solar orientation and a combination of glass and plastic cladding. These greenhouses also incorporate state-sponsored infrastructure that is not widely available on other farms, such as irrigation and power generation.

Spanish Name: *Agromercado* (See p. 113.)

English Name: Agricultural Markets

Date: Pre-1989

Number: N/A

Products: Vegetables, fruits, herbs, and value-added products, such as sauces; occasionally meats, eggs, and prepared foods

Purpose: To provide market goods for individuals

Elements: Tables or booths, usually with some tensile fabric overhead but generally open-air enterprises

Farmers: Farmers selling their own produce and vendors selling for farmers

Details: Urban markets are the primary source for fresh vegetables, herbs, meat, eggs, and fruit in Havana. These markets vary in size and shape but typically house multiple stalls—each with its own grower representatives—and occupy an existing building. Every neighborhood has a number of fresh markets, each with its own reputation resulting from the type and quality of the produce to cleanliness and affordablility.

Fresh food markets—although government sanctioned— are fundamentally different than the state-sponsored ration-based grocery stores in Havana and operate much like capitalistic entities. While the state-run farmers markets tend to be affordable, if uninspired, the popular free-markets offer better quality produce, with greater variety and slightly higher prices—out of reach for those who only get their state salary, but accessible for the many Cubans who have additional resources, such as remittances from the United States.

Almost all of the markets run by growers are housed in small lightweight, open-air structures. Some vegetables and fruit, as well as eggs and herbs, can also be found on the streets at informal mobile carts. Although all of these operations should be authorized by the Municipal Administration Council, the black market for food has also been a long-standing tradition in Havana.

Spanish Name: *Centros de Producción de Materia Orgánica* (See p. 114.)

English Name: Organic Matter Production Centers (composting centers)

Date started: 1999

Size: 10,000–20,000 sq. m. of land per center

Number: 12 UBPCs in all but 3 municipalities of Havana, 1 national center for research, and several mini-centers

Products: Soil, sometimes seedlings or saplings

Purpose: To provide organic compost or soil for farmers and urban gardeners

Elements: Separate soil beds for containing vermiculture, bags, and a sales area

Farmers: 5–6 people work at each center

Details: These composting centers collect, process, and distribute organic matter used for high-quality soil. About 15 percent of Havana's municipal waste is composted, including waste (e.g., rice husks and bagasse) from large dairy farms and agricultural-processing centers.

Micro-jardines / Micro-gardens

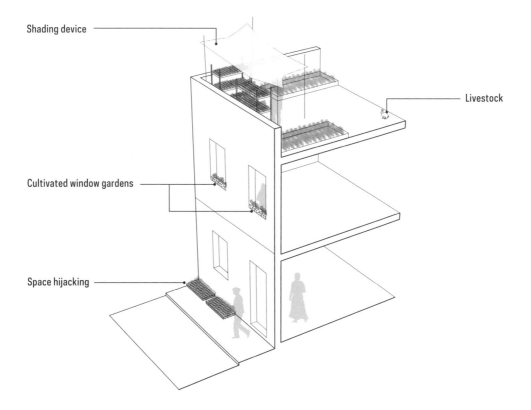

Shading device

Livestock

Cultivated window gardens

Space hijacking

Opposite, clockwise from top left: 1) A repurposed paint can used for growing 2) Tiny plants available for sale at a parcela 3) Pigs at a peri-urban farm 4) A balcony with small space for container gardening

Patios / Yards

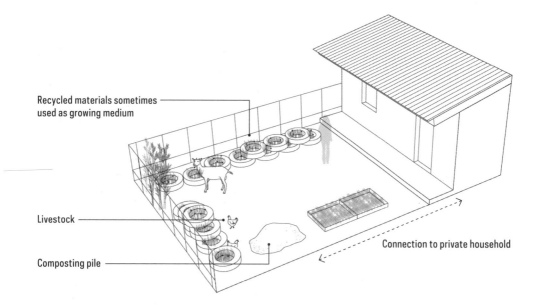

Recycled materials sometimes used as growing medium

Livestock

Composting pile

Connection to private household

Opposite, clockwise from top left: 1) **A small patio in Havana** *2)* **Chickens in an alley in the Vedado** *3)* **Rabbits in cages on a patio**

Parcelas / Lots

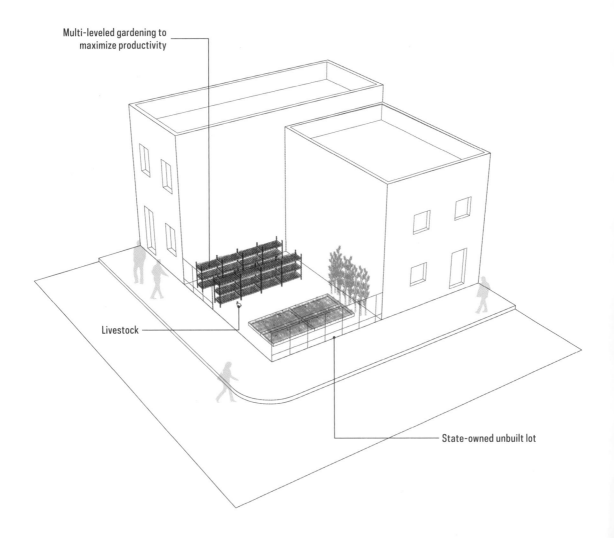

Multi-leveled gardening to maximize productivity

Livestock

State-owned unbuilt lot

Opposite, clockwise from top left: 1) The diverse plantings at a parcela, which was once a vacant lot used for dumping *2)* The organized, small-scale layout of a single-farmer parcela *3)* Parcela signage *4)* Concrete curbs are used for raised beds in a parcela.

Huertos Intensivos /
Intensive Cultivation Gardens

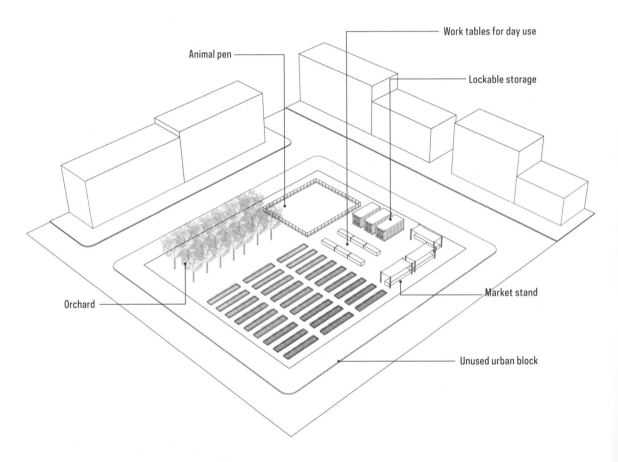

Work tables for day use

Animal pen

Lockable storage

Orchard

Market stand

Unused urban block

Opposite, clockwise from top left: 1) **Repurposed
roofing tiles make up the beds in this huerto intensivo.**
2) **At a huerto intensivo in the Parque Nacional
de Habana, raised beds are made of concrete curbs.**
3) **A farmer harvests produce at his huerto intensivo.**

Autoconsumos /
Self-provisioning Gardens

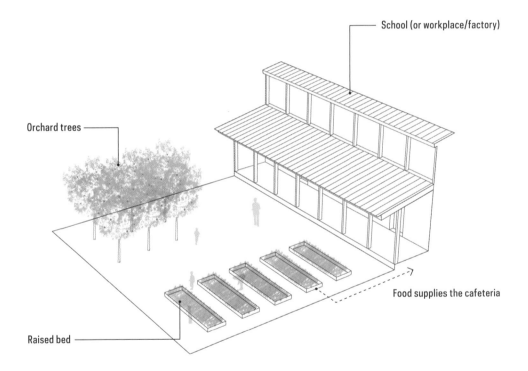

School (or workplace/factory)

Orchard trees

Food supplies the cafeteria

Raised bed

Opposite, clockwise from top left: 1) **A typical autoconsumo 2) A school garden, with a scarecrow and playground 3) Raised beds at an autoconsumo**

101

Organopónicos /
High-yield Urban Gardens

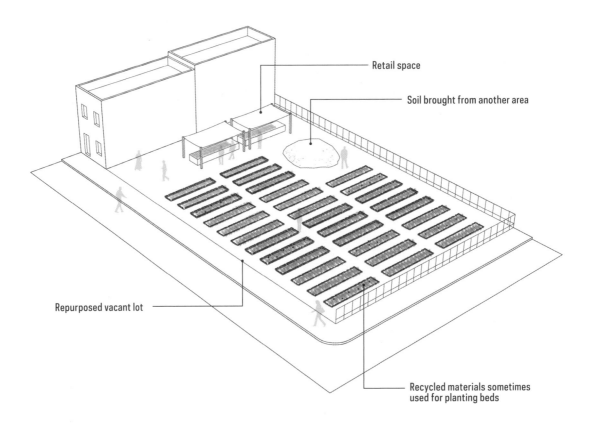

Retail space

Soil brought from another area

Repurposed vacant lot

Recycled materials sometimes
used for planting beds

Clockwise from top: 1) A tree nursery *2)* Raised beds made
from repurposed roofing tiles *3)* Worm humus, a product
created both to sell and for use

Campesinos Particulares / Private Peasant Gardens

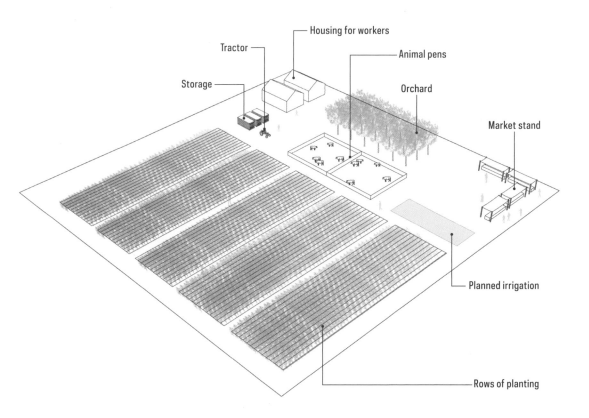

Housing for workers

Tractor

Animal pens

Orchard

Storage

Market stand

Planned irrigation

Rows of planting

Opposite, from top: 1) Intercropping of vegetables and orchard trees at a peri-urban farm *2)* Horses are still used by some farmers. *3)* Large, open fields and a crude fence define a peri-urban campesino farm. *4)* Cows at an organopónico

Empresas Estatales / State Enterprises

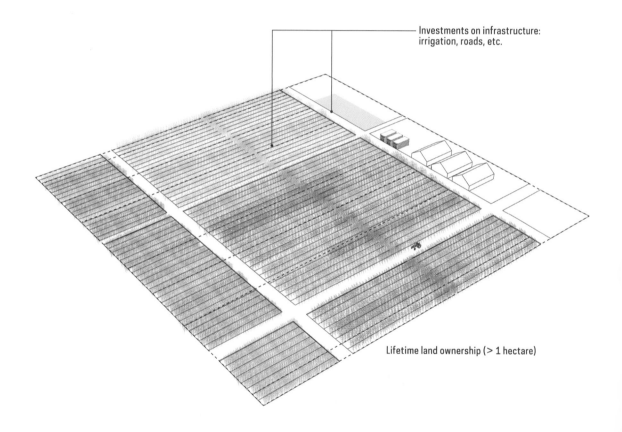

Investments on infrastructure: irrigation, roads, etc.

Lifetime land ownership (> 1 hectare)

Top: Tomatoes in a large greenhouse
Bottom: Cows graze at a large state farm.

Mataderos / Animal Husbandry

Above: Six farmers operate this large farm in Havana
with a variety of different animals. *Opposite, clockwise
from top left: 1)* Guinea pigs congregate on a rooftop
in the El Cerro neighborhood, where they can roam free.
2) The rabbits living on the rooftop feed the guinea
pigs that free range under them with their droppings.
3) Chickens in an alley in the Vedado. *4)* A goat tied
to a tree between the sidewalk and the street in the
Vedado. *5)* Honey harvest *6)* A cow at an organopónico.
7) Pigs raised at an independent urban farm.

Invernaderos /
Fresh Vegetable Greenhouses

Clockwise from top: 1) **Vegetables grown inside of a light-frame shade structure 2) Large greenhouses on an organopónico 3) A pass-through space for seedling trays keeps pests out**

Tiendas Consultorios Agropecuario / Agricultural Support Stores

Ornamental plants grown for sale to the public

Las Casas de Posturas / Seedling Greenhouses

Top: Seedlings in trays *Bottom:* An irrigation system at work

Agromercado / Agricultural Markets

Top: A downtown produce market. *Bottom:* On a street corner in the Vedado, a man sells onion braids.

Centros de Producción de Materia Orgánica / Organic Matter Production Centers

Clockwise from top: 1) A compost producer tends to beds where worms are grown for vermiculture. *2)* Worm humus, a product created both to sell and for use. *3)* At a small-scale compost center in Havana's Parque Metropolitano, bathtubs are used for vermiculture.

NOTES

1. Bourque and Rosset, "Lessons of Cuban Resistance," xviii.
2. In 2005 Bill McKibben called this the "world's largest model of a semi-sustainable agriculture." Bill McKibben, "The Cuba Diet," 62.
3. Berger defines the drosscape as "the inevitable wasted landscapes within urbanized areas that eternally elude the overly controlled parameters and the scripted programming elements that designers are charged with creating and accommodating in their projects." Alan Berger, *Drosscape: Wasting Land in Urban America*, (New York: Princeton Architectural Press, 2006), 12; See also Alan Berger, "Drosscape" in *The Landscape Urbanism Reader*, 199.
4. Peters, "Creating A Sustainable Urban Agricultural Revolution," 233-34.
5. The tourism sector is controlled by the government and has a distinct food allocation system that offers more diverse and high-quality products.

6. Wright, *Sustainable Agriculture and Food Security in an Era of Oil Scarcity*, 83, 188; Fernando Funes, "The Organic Farming Movement in Cuba," 18.
7. Infranet Lab/Lateral Office, "Formatting Contingency," *Pamphlet Architecture* 30, 9.
8. Cruz and Medina, *Agriculture in the City*, 176.
9. Premat, *Sowing Change*, 79, 106.
10. Funes et al., *Sustainable Agriculture and Resistance*, 220-36. In 2002 there were 104,087 patios and parcelas covering an area of 3,595 ha in Havana. Premat, *Sowing Change*, 85.
11. Ibid., 5.
12. Cruz and Medina, *Agriculture in the City*, 90.
13. Premat, *Sowing Change*, 56.
14. Cruz and Medina, *Agriculture in the City*, 30.
15. Dalia Acosta, "HEALTH-CUBA: Pigs Out of Havana, Orders Castro," *Inter Press Service*, March 12, 2002, http://ipsnews2.wpengine.com/2002/03/health-cuba-pigs-out-of-havana-orders-castro/
16. Rosset and Benjamin, *The Greening of the Revolution*, 25.

Gardens of Pleasure and Survival

Fritz Haeg

Why would someone grow his or her own food today? And what are the differences between those who do it out of necessity and those who do it by choice? These questions get at the heart of the cultural, economic, and social divides that have been complicating the conversations around food today. We see a spectrum of reasons for the rising interest in where our food is coming from and what we eat: Residents of urban-food deserts are growing fresh produce where it is not otherwise available. Victims of jobless economies and low wages, who cannot afford high grocery prices, might grow their own foods out of necessity. Prosperous, well-educated office workers, who are free to buy whatever they want, might choose to cultivate their own crops for pleasure, for the taste, or because of ethics or a general concern about the origins of what they find at the supermarket. Recent college graduates sizing up the world they have just entered may decide to start a vegetable garden as a form of resistance against the global industrial food complex.

    As an artist with a background in architecture, I am interested in making work that not only reflects but also participates in the realities of the world around me. I want to make work that is alive, changing, and engaged. I began as an amateur gardener when I moved to Los Angeles in 1999, finding myself continually drawn to gardens that were productive

Top: The small house in Budapest before planting
Bottom: Edible Estates garden number 12

in some way—gardens growing food that also happened to
be beautiful. In those gardens I recognized something significant,
urgent, and meaningful that I could not quite articulate at
the time.

My work gradually migrated away from architecture
and toward other forms of place-making activity, like gardens.
While searching for ways to consider environmental issues in
my work, it became clear that the domestic kitchen–garden was
the best model for how we could collectively relate to the land.
When you grow your own food, you become aware of closed
organic cycles and your place within them. You understand that
what you put into the soil and air outside your door will later
come inside and be consumed. A garden that grows food in the
city reminds us of hidden systems that support us. Gardening
is the easiest first wedge for any citizen—with access to a piece
of land—to physically make a mark on the city.

In 2005 I started a series of garden projects called
Edible Estates. Each garden is in a different city and typically
commissioned by a local museum or art institution. I work with
a family or community of households to create a highly visible
place in front of their house or apartment building to grow their
own food. Each garden is a prototype that demonstrates how
a typical urban resident might grow their own food where they
live. The locations are selected for their visibility, iconic qualities,
suitability for cultivation, and most importantly its potential
to be a provocative site for an edible garden. I have planted
twelve of these gardens so far, for a diverse range of families
in a variety of cities and living conditions, including a typical
middle-American home in Salina, Kansas, an apartment complex
in Austin, inner-city public housing in London, a suburban front
lawn in Los Angeles, a community center in Rome, and recently
a small house in a planned community in Budapest.

This endeavor is an art initiative outside of the obligations of commercial activity and public advocacy: The goal is not as simple as commercial viability or convincing people of the evils of lawns and virtues of gardens. When questions come up about the intelligence of growing food in cities with polluted air and soil, perhaps we can turn the question back on itself and ask why the air and soil are polluted. When we complain that we do not have time to grow our own food, we can refer to statistics about the time people spend online, watching television, or sitting in traffic. When we acknowledge that we cannot solve the global food problems with little kitchen gardens, that understanding leads us down a road of inquiry. With each garden I have encountered successes and failures that have illuminated realities of contemporary urban life.

In Salina, Kansas, in 2005 I was lucky enough to plant a garden for Stan Cox, a plant biologist at the nearby Land Institute. His enthusiasm, gardening skills, plant expertise, and access to particular species suitable to the extreme prairie climate made his house the perfect site for the first garden. The garden continues today as a wild but well-tended space for he and his wife to grow food not available at their local markets. They are actively political people, critical of many aspects of contemporary capitalist society and eager to advocate for radical changes—and the garden is clearly the most public and visible announcement of this desire.

In 2006 the Foti family of Lakewood, California, was already cultivating raised beds of vegetables in the backyard as well as a few hens that provided eggs. The couple had both grown up in this suburban community and appreciated it enough to stay and raise their own family there. Because of their love for their city, they were adamant about not wanting to disrespect or upset their neighbors with the new garden, which we knew would raise some eyebrows. In those first weeks of the garden, it did. They recounted an elderly couple who would intentionally walk by each evening and shake their heads in disgust as they passed. Other neighbors, when questioned by a *New York Times* reporter, expressed concern about the negative effect on property values—and even about vegetable thieves. As the neighbors watched the family work and saw the garden grow through the season, I think most of those concerns abated.

In 2007, I planted a new frontyard garden for a family in the respectable commuter town of Maplewood, New Jersey. One neighbor hated the garden, thinking it was ugly, wild, and a sign of anarchy; each new animal that would show up in the garden was evidence to her that things on her street were unraveling, thanks to this new garden. On the other hand, the elderly German immigrant neighbor on the other side welcomed it as a nice addition to the street—a sign of progress. The husband, a chef, and his wife were interested in nutrition for their son but were also serious foodies. The couple was starting a new baby-food business. The decision to dramatically and publicly grow so much of their own food came from an interest in and enjoyment of good food, accompanied by an activist desire to shift societal values, at least a bit.

At the council housing estates in London, only two adult residents turned up for a planting weekend in 2007 to help local volunteers, but there was a flood of children. (This was the case everywhere I went. From Salina to Austin, as soon as the dirt, plants, and shovels showed up and work began, it was hard to keep the kids away.) The particular children at the London garden have continued to be involved in the life of the garden, if not helping with the work, at least keeping tabs on its progress and nibbling on the output throughout the seasons.

A couple of years later the garden had established itself as a visible fixture on the street, and passersby could watch crops go through the seasonal cycle. And although the residents were resistant to a composting system when we first planted the garden, eventually a composting system was established for the entire building. Many local residents were participating in modest ways—setting out a few plants in the communal garden—but Denise was the resident who ultimately made the garden possible. She had been depressed and unemployed and had never gardened a day in her life when we first met. She was thoroughly committed from the beginning and became the definitive force behind its continued growth and success. She tended to it daily, welcomed in the kids to help, and was eventually hired by the nonprofit urban-greening organization that managed the project. I'm sure that diets changed and the land was revived with activity, but the most powerful outcome was that just a few local residents were given a space out their door to make their mark on their community and city.

I decided on the neighborhood of Wekerle in Budapest as the site for a prototype garden in 2012. This early-twentieth-century planned community, inspired by Ebenezer Howard's Garden City, was designed to house the rural farmers who had come to the city for factory jobs. They would feel at home in the romantic, village-like suburb, the vernacular style of which was intended to remind them of the villages they had left behind. With each dwelling designed to include land for residents to cultivate their own food, they would also be able to continue to use their farming skills. There are stories of each family being provided with four fruit trees when they moved in and bumper currant crops covering their housing costs.

Today, however, Wekerle is a World Heritage Site, which prohibits any radical change to the visible designs, including—

ironically—the addition of visible kitchen gardens. In fact, the owners and I needed to schedule a special last-minute meeting with the mayor of Kispest to get permission to plant our garden. He threw his support behind us, and even showed up with his son to help plant. I found an absence of a culture of aesthetically pleasing food growing in Hungary: either a garden is beautiful and ornamental or ugly and productive. For the many Hungarians I spoke with, gardening and getting your hands in the dirt to grow your own food was not considered romantic or aspirational. Despite having emerged from the Soviet bloc decades ago, there still is the desire to catch up on all of the material pleasures they missed out on—and farming is something you leave behind to get there.

The family said they were eager to have the garden to promote a better diet for their daughter, but I later discovered that they did not encourage her to help out. Perhaps they thought getting her hands in the dirt would be a step backward for their only child, who they hope to give opportunities they did not have. They soon realized how much work the garden would be and, overwhelmed by the hours, leaned heavily on the nearby grandmothers to pitch in. After a last interview with the family at the end of the first season of the garden, I realized that their motivations might have been mostly financial. They were scraping by on just enough to make ends meet, and the opportunity to grow food in the vast expanse of dirt outside their door was too good to pass up. Why were they not growing food there before? And will they continue the garden next year?

Support

WHILE FARMS AND GARDENS OCCUPY THE SPATIAL, VISUAL, and organizational center of Havana's urban agriculture movement, their success rests on the efforts of a host of support services. Much of this support is institutional: State-sponsored advocacy groups promote animal husbandry, permaculture, and agricultural research. The government also provides training and materials, access points for agricultural services, and the legal framework to facilitate land acquisition. Without this critical backing, city growers would not have realized the overwhelming success and widespread agricultural improvement that has emerged over the years. In facilitating urban farming efforts, support groups have effectively raised the bar for standard agricultural practice in Cuba, primarily by promoting and disseminating advanced farming methods.

Research labs are currently creating new organic pesticides, plant varieties, and veterinary medicines, all of which are affordable and accessible to growers through a national network of providers. Throughout the country, centers—known as CREES—for the production of *entomophages* (organisms that eat insects) and *entomopathogens* (organisms that cause disease in insects) develop and manufacture small-scale biological control agents.[1] Although developed by scientists, these products are refined and perfected by trying new approaches, testing new ideas, and reaching out to practitioners—farmers and gardeners—for resources and ideas, in an example of the critical (and formal) feedback loop between the government and the grower.[2]

Much of the innovation related to urban agriculture in Havana has relied on coordination between state-sponsored institutions and organizations. One original land-use strategy—born out of the Special Period—was a rise in dual-use facilities for production in a space-saving, resource-sharing model. For example, the thirty brewer's yeast factories in Cuba, which produce yeast just several days during the month, were converted to production centers for government-sponsored commercial-scale biopesticides during their idle days.[3]

The Cuban Ministry of Agriculture (MINAG) controls the direction of the urban agriculture movement and has used its vision to highlight strategic programs at specific times. For instance, in 2000, MINAG worked on a fruit-tree campaign that created new tree nurseries, trained urban tree stewards, and also provided citrus-tree seedlings throughout MINAG branches as a protected product. This coordinated effort resulted in the large-scale improvement of the urban citrus-tree canopy. Given MINAG's broad reach, one focused program can have an enormous physical, social, and environmental impact, resulting in new trends that ultimately generate city form.

Outreach and training is a primary source of support for growers, provided by many different organizations to varying degrees. MINAG representatives make field visits to urban sites during which they recruit new farmers to convert their own rooftops, balconies, and yards for productive agricultural uses, as well as offer on-site support to existing farmers. These experts, based out of extension offices in thirteen of the fifteen municipalities in Havana and employed by the government, provide free education and support services to urban farmers. While these programs tend to prioritize quantity over quality— MINAG focuses on growing their participation numbers—they do improve information access through their field visits, annual award programs, and collaborations with the news media.

The Cuban Organic Farming Association also hosts workshops, field tours, lectures, and meetings with farmers to disseminate information. One of their programs includes a mobile agroecological library that moves from production sites to educational centers and institutions to make the resources

Top: Biopesticides in jars. *Bottom*: A biopesticide expert applies his own artisanal biopesticide on crops.

readily available. National exchange programs, the development
of agricultural curriculum, access to shared resources—such as
libraries, articles, conferences, and workplace development—
also provide growers with opportunities for learning. Even
so-called unconventional programs have garnered the support
of the state: For example, the *Fundacion Antonio Núñez Jiménez
de la Naturaleza y el Hombre* sponsors permaculture workshops
in Havana, in which they have trained more than three hundred
producers and technicians to date.[4]

Government incentives have also helped to reintegrate
farming into Cuban culture. One of the first programs—
popularized in the 1960s—was voluntary agricultural service

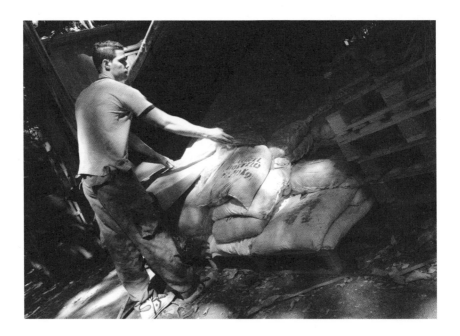

A compost producer stacks bags of organic soil to be sold.

(for a duration between two weeks and two years), in which urban dwellers were paired with farms or gardens. This work-study initiative, known as the National Food Program, has been one method employed by the government in an effort to reverse rural-urban demographic shifts. This training has since been bolstered by incentives such as the provision of attractive new housing for rural and peri-urban farmers: In 1990 approximately one hundred fifty thousand Habaneros participated.[5] While this program has prompted some urban dwellers to move to the countryside with fresh skills and the promise of a better quality of life, it has also trained a new corps of city growers.

Despite overwhelming social and political support, most Cuban gardeners lack the economic resources needed to buy even the most basic tools, and many small-scale farmers work without important infrastructural systems. Built infrastructure, such as windmills, wells, irrigation systems, rainwater catchment, greenhouses, compost areas, spaces for tool storage, animal production facilities, and, in the city, connections to recycling and waste streams, often requires a level of economic investment that is out of reach to citizen farmers. Even soil may need to be purchased and brought to the site by hand, a process that for some can take many hundreds of loads.

Community Engagement

The Revolution brought new life to Cuban values, central to which was the equitable division of resources and agricultural accessibility for all. This ethic continues to inform Cuban agriculture today, principally as an open invitation for citizens to participate in the urban farming movement regardless of gender, age, or race.[6] Many farmers arrive at their profession via university training in other disciplines; the country's guaranteed education system has produced an unusually large cadre of intellectual farmers. It is not uncommon to meet full-time farmers in Cuba who have PhDs, or are licensed engineers or certified technicians. Perhaps it is because of this intersection of agriculture and education that Cuban farmers regularly work to solve agricultural problems jointly with scientists. Farmers are highly regarded in Cuba, and because of the semi-open food market, farmers earn some of the highest salaries in the city.

Many of the agricultural resources provided by the state are disseminated through community and neighborhood

Farmers prepare dried herbs for sale on an organopónico.

associations. Early in the development of the Cuban urban farming program, the government established a number of group-growing intiatives to help alleviate the daunting task of educating thousands of new farmers. For example, the fresh-vegetable producer clubs that started in the early 1990s have since been sanctioned by the government and continue to train and support new farmers using government supplied materials. Today these popular associations are called Farmers Groups, hosting between fifteen and twenty people per club in neighborhoods throughout Havana. These growers' clubs—combined with shared farming models, tool-share programs, and training facilities—scale even individual urban farms up to that of the block or neighborhood.

Cubans hail urban agriculture as a boon for the community, occasionally in too-idealistic terms. Cuban media and government publications focus almost exclusively on the positive elements of the initiative, and literature reinforces these propagandistic messages claiming, for example, that "by promoting urban farming, cities and their surrounding areas can be made virtually self-sufficient in perishable foods, be beautified, and have greater employment opportunities."[7] However, with experience and widespread community engagement, urban growers have found their own reasons to participate. Access to and control over an independent food source ranks high among the reasons for many to farm inside the city; incentives also include a higher social status, gratifying work, and competitive salaries. Both the state and citizens benefit from employment opportunities created by urban agriculture, which, according to agricultural ecologist Richard Levins, "creates employment at about twenty jobs per hectare."[8]

In the case of Havana, urban farming may be a by-product of socialism; the appropriation of space for communal farming tends to reinforce a socialist ethic. Cuban ideology regarding self-sufficiency, such as the firmly held belief that individuals should know what is involved in the production of the goods they consume, thoroughly permeates the society. As a result, it is natural for people to be interested in participating in farming practices and for many citizens to have a good working knowledge of agricultural systems. This ethic is built into the state-sponsored education system, etched into Cuban culture, and honed by the tradition of volunteer service on farms.

Government Involvement

Having effectively nationalized every aspect of life on the island, the post-revolution Cuban government created a monopoly on food access that made its citizens wholly dependent on the state for survival. When the food crisis occurred in the late 1980s, both the legitimacy and the efficacy of this socialist system were put to the test. The Cuban government responded with unconventional and unprecedented changes to this system, not the least of which was a willingness to allow individuals to manage their own food access—and in some cases, profit by it— which marked an important shift in power in the early 1990s.[9]

Most of the state-supported urban farming initiatives were introduced from a state-centered socialist platform. In 1991, at the fifth congress of the Cuban Association of Agricultural and Forestry Technicians, Fidel Castro expressed an intention to "convert farming into one of the most honored, promoted, and appreciated professions."[10] In the following years, urban agriculture gained the complete support of the state and was considered a critical solution to widespread hunger.[11]

This political response to food insecurity also inculcated an attitude of perseverance under adversity, namely through the propaganda and cutbacks initiated during the Special Period.

Fidel Castro declared that the country's agricultural "problems must be resolved without feedstock, fertilizers or fuel;" and in 1994 Raúl Castro reminded the country that "the central strategic, economic, political, ideological, and military task for all Cuban revolutionaries, without exception, is to guarantee the population's food supply."[12] These types of entreaties characterized the leanest years in Cuba and the desperate tenor of that period demonstrates the powerful motivation that led political leaders to entertain alternative solutions.

The spatial reallocation of farmland in Cuba was addressed—physically and politically—through a synergistic relationship that served as a catalyst for the widespread

Rice delivery to a government ration store downtown

133

adoption of the citizen-farmer movement. The common refrain
during the Special Period—that "no space in the city should
go uncultivated"—was made possible by the assurance of free
government-supplied land for every individual who wanted
to farm.[13] Fidel Castro redistributed as much as two-thirds of
state lands to cooperatives and individual farmers during this
time. The Cuban government's facilitation of urban farming
efforts also assumed nonphysical forms, highlighting the value
of positive national press, lenient agricultural directives, and
party endorsement to accelerate and energize the movement.
For instance, Raúl Castro instituted the National Day for
Urban Agriculture on December 27, 1997, and it continues
to be recognized today.[14] The government provides loans for
some farm types, such as state-sponsored organopónicos with
favorable rates and conditions. NGOs also assist small urban
farms, minimizing their restrictions and interference in an
effort to facilitate additional aid. Since 2000, foreign financing
through NGOs has been an important source of funding
for small community gardens to purchase tools, irrigation,
buildings, well-drilling assistance, windmills, and seeds,
as well as new technologies and greenhouses.

The long tenure of the government has ensured the
lasting impact of these visionary programs: According to
scholar Charles Lesher, the laws that make this kind of urban
planning successful are inextricably linked to stable, visionary,
and supportive leadership.[15] Indeed, Cuba's robust urban
agriculture network could not exist without this political
support. Despite Cuba's fervent endorsement of the movement
today, party leaders have not always championed this mode
of food production. In the early 1990s, officials worried that
self-provisioning would encourage independent or subversive
civic action and that urban farming practices would need large

degrees of control and supervision. Despite its enthusiastic sponsorship of farming initiatives, growers point out that the government remains inconsistent in its support, providing only short-term land tenure for farmers and setting animal-husbandry allowances that can fluctuate at a moment's notice.

Overall, however, the collective action and united support for urban food production in Cuba stands in stark contrast to the position of many other countries, where urban farming initiatives are dampened by planning processes and government figures or individuals who do not share the same vision. The widespread support of the government both facilitates farming efforts and provides Habaneros with a vehicle for engaged citizenship. Adriana Premat's decade-long interviews with Cuban growers, documented in *Sowing Change*, have demonstrated that "the political pedigree of such urban agriculture sites was often mentioned in the media and was common knowledge among urban agriculture practitioners."[16] Whether on usufruct lands, through state-sponsored farming initiatives, or on their own patios, Habaneros have realized that state affirmation can be a very useful tool. This government approval translates to awards and recognition from the media; access to foreign visitors who may offer gifts; resources from NGOs; and less scrutiny for minor offenses, such as having pigs in parts of the city where they are banned.

Cuban agricultural propaganda serves on both an instructive and didactic level. Citizens respond enthusiastically to socialist directives, and the dissemination of agricultural information tends to be far more effective when a single-party perspective monopolizes media coverage. The widespread and unrelenting press devoted to self-provisioning has undoubtedly bolstered urban farming efforts in Havana. However, the Cuban government can also obstruct research and warp data: It is likely that MINAG overstates food production rates and that farmers stock their gardens with animals and plants specifically for visiting tour groups. Regardless, Cuba's government involvement also demonstrates to the rest of the world a rare level of political participation: Raúl Castro typically attends the annual meeting on the state of urban agriculture, and the government publishes an annual report card for each city, ensuring that urban agriculture maintains a high public profile.

Urban agriculture has flourished in Havana under extraordinary state support and assistance with programs and resources. However, this movement also reveals the state's inability to provide food security to its citizens through more

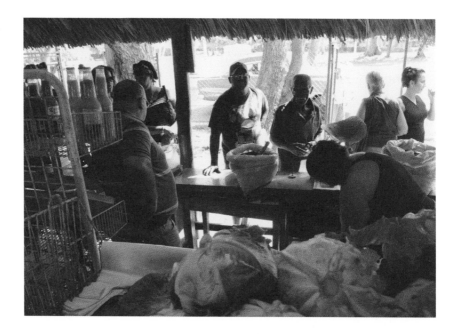

Vendors sell produce and value-added goods to the public at an organopónico farm stand.

traditional modes of practice, and, in this respect, signals
a breakdown in the government's absolute power structure.
Ultimately, urban farming efforts in Cuba represent a people's
movement, highlighting the community's ability to take care
of itself in periods of uncertainty, and even crisis.

Havana's urban farms embody this participatory shift and
may even represent subversive action in their new appropriation
of communal space. In doing so, the simple act of gardening
could be understood as a form of insurgent citizenship,
articulated by anthropologist James Holston in his 1995 essay
"Spaces of Insurgent Citizenship." Here gardens represent
"sites of insurgence because they introduce into the city new
identities and practices that disturb established histories."[17]
The ground-up, engaged action exhibited in Havana parallels
normative Western thinking about the food-justice movement:
One challenges the corporate, market-responsive, and large-
scale system of food production (common in North America),
both in terms of food access and security. Cuba's community-
based model, comparatively "revolutionary, subversive, and
necessarily the open-source, chaotic, decentralized nature of the
urban-agriculture revolution," presents another option.[18]

Havana's urban agriculture program occupies a political
and social middle ground, fueled by government initiatives but
powered by an organized and collaborative group of growers.
On one hand, it began as a movement characterized by people
bringing animals and vegetables closer to their own tables; on
the other hand, it has become a movement popularized by the
press, and guided by the state and an assembly of organized
infrastructures, replete with a formal bureaucracy and official
regulations. As it stands, this network relies on both formal
and informal modes of action: It is a product of seed banks and
rotating veterinarians, of space hijacking, and free markets.

Beyond the Green Revolution

Prior to the 1989 food crisis, Cuba's agricultural development prioritized technological progress and scientific prowess over citizen engagement, in an agricultural model based on Green Revolution principles. When this system failed, the government immediately grasped the need for a more resilient agricultural model and embraced the opportunity to approach agricultural production at the small-scale, community level. This transition from Green Revolution agricultural principles to a more socialist agricultural platform also signaled a shift toward a more sustainable model of food production in Cuba.

Unlike the Green Revolution, in which technology served as the primary means for agricultural improvement, Cuba's post-oil model stressed the importance of social and political transformation. In keeping with revolutionary ideas, programs linked agriculture to social change. Despite this enlightened social approach, it must be remembered that the Cuban model showcases an innovative and progressive relationship between community engagement and agricultural technologies against a backdrop of political persecution and human-rights violations.

Agricultural advances and social change have long been intertwined in Cuba's state identity. From revolutionary and poet José Martí's visionary self-sufficiency ethic to Fidel Castro's defiant response to trade embargos, farming has come to represent more than just an effort to put food on the table. Urban farming, according to Richard Levins, is inextricably linked to state power systems, where "Cuban agriculture is a socialist agriculture, created under difficult conditions to meet socialist goals."[19] Since 1989, Havana's growers have responded to resource scarcity in political terms, creating what Levins calls a new "socialist ecology, a socialist pattern of relations between humans and the land, the insects, the fungi, and tomatoes."[20]

NOTES

1. Rosset and Benjamin, *The Greening of the Revolution*, 41. Two hundred eighteen of these centers had been deployed across Cuba by 1992.
2. Ibid., 77.
3. Ibid., 41-42.
4. Cruz and Medina, *Agriculture in the City*, 182.
5. Schultz, "Food Sovereignty and Cooperatives in Cuba's Socialism," 127.
6. More men than women choose to participate in Cuban urban agriculture, but both genders are equally allowed and encouraged, including in taking on leadership positions.
7. Bourque and Rosset, "Lessons of Cuban Resistance," xix.
8. Richard Levins "The Unique Pathway of Cuban Development," 278.
9. Premat, *Sowing Change*, 9.
10. Rosset and Benjamin, *The Greening of the Revolution*, 33.
11. Not the least of this support was the creation of an urban agriculture department by the Cuban Ministry of Agriculture for Havana's city government.
12. Rosset and Benjamin, *The Greening of the Revolution*, 33; Raúl Castro, "Speech given by Raúl Castro," *Granma International*, August 17, 1994, 12.
13. Murphy, "Cultivating Havana," 1.
14. González Novo et al., *Testimonios*, 25.
15. Charles W. Lesher, Jr., "Urban Agriculture: A Literature Review: Urban Agriculture: Differing Phenomena in Differing Regions of the World" (Master's thesis, Tulane University, Fall 2006).
16. Premat, *Sowing Change*, 31.
17. James Holston, ed., *Cities and Citizenship* (Durham, N.C.: Duke University Press Books, 1998), 167.
18. Cockrall-King, *Food and the City*, 17.
19. Levins, "The Unique Pathway of Cuban Development," 277.
20. Ibid.

Evolving Design Roles

Jorge Peña Díaz

After more than two decades, Cuba's urban and peri-urban agriculture movement remains strong and has shown signs of positive growth. The Cuban food crisis has practically disappeared, yet citywide production and yields continue to grow. This production number surpassed one million tons of city-grown food in 2012, making up around 10 percent of Cuba's overall food production.[1] Moreover, the territory allocated to urban agriculture—in all its forms—has steadily continued to grow. All municipalities have developed individual urban farming programs in spite of the pressures of urbanization. The number of people earning their income from urban agriculture–related food production and the share of the contribution of these farms to daily diets is very likely to have increased as well. Meanwhile, the particular arrangement of raised beds associated with organopónicos—one of the most visible and recognizable forms—have become a natural part of the urban landscape.

Cuba's urban agriculture has become one of the most well-known and respected models for food security and has had a tremendous impact abroad. These lessons translate to other regions and across a wide variety of disciplines, from scholars to social and environmental activists. Not surprisingly, many international research and design projects have found inspiration in this initiative, yielding a host of rich and varied proposals for the future global city.

In the case of Cuba, however, this agricultural production was not the result of conscious urban landscape strategies generated by urban design offices. Rather, it was a movement derived from the disciplined implementation of agricultural practice and dictated by the functional requirements of food production in such a setting. Design decisions— such as the appropriate width for raised beds—came from the need to provide access to farmers and to accommodate the rotation of specific vegetables throughout the year. The orientation of these beds ensures sufficient sunlight, the location of protective plants reveals a strategy to confuse pests, and the arrangement of trees within the garden provides shaded areas for the production of worm humus. All of these technical considerations have generated a specific kind of farming landscape that has been replicated all over the country—namely because these standardized design suggestions have been formalized and distributed by the state.

Outside of Cuba, landscape architects and urban designers willingly engage urban agriculture as an urban-intervention strategy. For example, a 2012 exhibition in Cologne entitled *Productive Urban Landscapes* assembled fourteen agricultural projects from landscape-architecture and urban design studios. Such an initiative exposes the popularity of urban agriculture and highlights a willingness among urban designers to appropriate this thinking into their practice. Urban agriculture—a practice that has had specific sociocultural and economic roots in these territories—has been ushered into the public arena by the hand of planners and designers, who have created a design-driven perspective for the new green mainstream.

In spite of its comprehensive and sophisticated development of urban agriculture, planning and design have had a different role in the case of Cuba. In order to comprehend this distinctive approach, it is necessary to understand two driving forces that directly impact a country in which more than 75 percent of the population lives in urban settlements. First, the extraordinary food-production model generated by urban agriculture was actually a reaction to the disorder of the entire urban food system. Secondly, Cuba's urbanization process over the last fifty years has defined unique patterns that affect urban agriculture. These two elements frame the context within which Cuban planners and designers must work.

Necessity pushed Cuba to adopt a largely agroecological approach to food production and urban agriculture became a primary means of feeding urban dwellers. The food crisis of 1989 not only affected agricultural production in the countryside but also had the concomitant effect of limiting transportation into cities. Agricultural support facilities became inoperable, and energy scarcity limited the capacity of agricultural and food-processing plants. Even consumers had difficulty accessing goods from established vendors.

A combination of social innovation and political will has allowed for the development of urban agriculture, the latter appearing to be the single key factor in guaranteeing the program's longevity. Cuba's urban farming program was triggered by the need to reduce the oversized food-importation bill that makes Cuba a "net importer…dependent financially from other sectors of the economy."[2] This network of gardens and farms has continued to grow; in 2009 the creation of a new economic program to specifically address peri-urban agriculture demonstrated a considerable increase in urban farmland. Facilitating the access to land at the peripheries of municipalities is just one example of the ways in which the program has been supported by new laws promoting the conversion of idle into productive land.

The extent of this support for urban farming was exemplified by its inclusion in the guidelines for the economic and social development of the country approved by the Sixth Congress of the Communist Party in 2011. Within these guidelines, the chapter devoted to agriculture is the single largest one, making up more than 10 percent of the total volume. Two specific guidelines have been devoted to urban agriculture in this document, pointing to the favorable framework that has been emerged in support of urban agriculture during the past two decades.

Havana provides a case study for understanding the second factor that impacted the development of urban farming in Cuba. Unlike its neighbors, Havana's population growth has stagnated. While the highly educated population ages, the occupation of the neighborhoods has waned, and the expansion of the city's boundaries remains close to those conceived in 1958. The original urban fabric of Havana has been preserved, and there is no aggressive real estate market defining the rules of land value. Urban agriculture has found a niche as a result of a shrinking urbanization model and culture, and this low competition atmosphere explains why urban agriculture has managed to integrate so seamlessly with other urban functions.

In addition to these two driving factors, the presence of urban agriculture in the Cuban media has guaranteed its visibility to the average citizen, resulting in increased accountability of lawmakers. Trimestral evaluations by the National Urban Agriculture Group of each municipality are broadcasted on television and reported in detail by the most important newspapers. Municipalities and popular councils with poor agricultural production performances are given a negative mark. Other aspects of urban agriculture—aesthetics, economic, and environmental issues—tend to have a lower public profile. For instance, discussions of a farm or garden's contextual response to "the urban" is often limited to the quality of the fences; in conversations about urban farming, "it is notable… that design considerations receive very little attention."[3]

In spite of the current economic improvements, the impact of the crisis stymied several components of the urban food system, which also remained dependent on external factors, such as trade capacity. Additionally, conventional farming has not yet returned to pre-1989 standards; perhaps due in part to the success of urban farming.

Planning has made significant contributions to urban agriculture throughout the years, since planners were instrumental in the original identification of suitable locations for farms. This role has grown with the inclusion of urban agriculture as a permanent function in Havana's Master Plan in 2000. Currently the planning system is in charge of processing agricultural land. However, in spite of this critical supporting role, the planning profession has remained essentially reactive toward urban agriculture, and control-oriented approaches have prevailed.

Today there is an intensive ongoing debate between planners, urban designers, and architects on the role that cities will play in Cuba's future socioeconomic scenarios. The debate, however, has not been accompanied by the materialization of projects that mirror their proponents' views. No critical mass of either urban or architectural works can demonstrate where and how society evaluates the spatial qualities of this type of vision.

The adaptation of agriculture into urban planning has been caught in the same trap. There are virtually no built examples of proposals from planners, urban designers, or architects in which urban agriculture forms a part of a landscape strategy. There have been no proposals promoting synergies with other components of the urban fabric in more than two decades of urban-agriculture development. This is true for both land-use planning and for integration into urban-design schemes, in spite of the fact that there is a relevant antecedent in the Green Belt, or Cordón de La Habana, on the outskirts of Havana that integrated food production, leisure, and landscaping.

On one hand, this may reflect the visibility of risks associated with urban agriculture independent of its positive impacts. But it also demonstrates that architects and planners feel unfamiliar with aspects of urban agriculture, which might prevent more proactive behavior. Planners and landscape architects have successfully established many innovative approaches toward urban agriculture in cities with far less urban agriculture experience than Havana. Yet in Cuba this type of relationship remains almost unexplored. The demands and the driving forces of the urban food system, including its technical requirements, have instead generated the unique landscape associated with urban agriculture.

Design is likely to have a different role in cities worldwide, depending on the evolution of the urban-food system toward a new equilibrium, which will need to shift to ensure food security. Furthermore, this design thinking will develop in parallel with changes in the urbanization process. Design has the opportunity to become the primary tool for integrating the food-related and spatial demands of a new urban scenario, currently only in its nascent stage.

NOTES

1. INIFAT Grupo Nacional de Agricultura Urbana, "Principales tareas desarrolladas en el año 2009," in *Agricultura Urbana Boletin Informativo*, (January 1, 2010): 2.

2. Partido Comunista de Cuba, *Lineamientos de La Política Económica y Social de La Revolución y El Partido* (Havana: Cuban Communist Party, 2011).

3. Jorge Peña Díaz, *Contribución a la integración de la agricultura urbana y peri urbana en el plan de ordenamiento territorial y el urbanismo en los municipios de Ciudad Habana* (Havana: Instituto Superior Politécnico José Antonio Echeverría, 2005).

Designing and Planning

Chapter 4

CUBA'S FOOD CRISIS HIGHLIGHTED MANY OF THE DEEPLY
entrenched and largely invisible structural problems within
the country's food system. Flaws in agricultural infrastructure,
community-engagement process, modes of knowledge transfer,
production methods, and urban planning were plainly exposed
with the dissolution of the Soviet bloc. Architectural theorist
Mark Wigley links these larger systems failures to design,
suggesting that these "crises always appear as the failure of a
spatial system, a failure of architecture."[1] In this sense, periods
of extreme breakdown can also act as agents of physical change:
according to Wigley, "crises produce new forms."[2]

While urban planning would ideally engage agricultural
opportunities well in advance of food shortages, in the case
of Cuba these efforts were applied across the city's fabric as
a response to real needs. From an urban design perspective,
many of these agricultural interventions in Havana continue
to remain disassociated from their physical context, lacking
linkages that could be made with built elements, comprehensive
signage, or other synergistic design responses. The formal
implications of urban agriculture could be used constructively,
perhaps even sustaining or branding within the larger urban
planning work in Havana. This shift in thinking—from
the strictly functional urban farm to the revered cultural
landscape—would necessarily need to draw insight from both
growers and designers. Planner and permaculture activist
María Caridad Cruz acknowledges that this collaboration is a
challenging yet essential undertaking, and that "inserting urban
agriculture into the land-management system is not a task
to be worked out on a drawing board." Instead, she writes, "it
depends, to a great extent, on the interrelation among planners
and doers, the community, and governments."[3] Indeed,
Fidel Castro's ability to seamlessly embed agriculture within

Cuba's political and social context has not given rise to an associated design cohesion, despite the potential to link farms to neighborhoods through physical and spatial planning. The communication breakdown between design and agricultural professionals in Cuba appears to be a missed opportunity.

From the scale of individual farm components to the much larger systems that define growing spaces, design could serve to frame and contextualize the discussion around Havana's agricultural infrastructure. Whether formally designed or not, growing spaces affect urban identity and have attendant shaping power, becoming part of the anatomy of the city. According to architect and educator Keller Easterling, some "of the most radical changes to the globalizing world are being written about not in the language of law and diplomacy, but rather in a spatial language of infrastructure."[4] Design thinking at this level also scales up to urban and regional planning, where infrastructural changes might begin to have profound impacts on the larger foodshed.

Havana's urban agriculture movement has been criticized as being a utilitarian and reactionary response to food scarcity rather than a proactive urban design initiative. Many of the state-sanctioned permanent farms in Havana occurred opportunistically in the decade following the food crisis, using land that was available rather than appropriate. Adriana Premat points to the informal space appropriation that growers employed in Havana, noting that "organopónicos have been built just because there was a nook here, a vacant lot there, even though they broke up the normal flow of city streets."[5] Landscapes that might otherwise have been slated for more conventional uses—parking lots, playgrounds, city parks, rooftops, and front yards—transitioned into a new agricultural terrain for food production.

Top: A rooftop garden as seen from the street.
Bottom: Crumbling buildings provide balcony and
rooftop growing spaces.

Because food access was such a dire and immediate need in Cuba, urban agriculture was prioritized over many other important uses, including environmental stewardship, housing development, and the formation of public recreation spaces. Urban agriculture initiatives have occasionally prevented the development or retention of valued civic amenities, such as parks. This collective tunnel vision has led to a divide between agricultural advocates and other types of developers, "pitt[ing] those involved in city planning and renovation against key decision makers in the Urban Agriculture Department and the armed forces, whose primary concern was food production rather than good urban design."[6] Despite the regular interweaving of agriculture with buildings and other types of spaces, there is still a perception by designers and planners that food production has unfairly taken precedence over housing and recreational spaces in urban areas. This interlacing is evident in most of Havana's neighborhoods, with the exception of the historic *Habana Vieja* district, where development for tourism has all but eliminated the last two decades of urban agriculture efforts.

Despite the popularity of urban farming in Havana, arguments against the practice still surface. For these trained planners, government officials, and residents, agriculture in the city is seen as an inappropriate use of public space or a stopgap measure that would prove unsustainable in the long term. One urban planner agreed that "urban agriculture is a city function, like housing, but gardens should be properly designed," while other Habaneros simply do not view farming as an appropriate piece of the contemporary city.[7] According to Premat, "those with official jurisdiction over the design and development of urban space rejected the notion of bringing food production into core municipalities because such activities were considered unsightly and out of place, particularly in the capital."[8] And as in the rest of North America, there remains a real cultural divide between the design community and the growers themselves: "Cubans are very pragmatic, emphasizing usefulness. Planners and architects are trained otherwise, and the stigma of urban farming is maintained."[9]

Urban farming has not been wholeheartedly embraced by the Cuban design community—perhaps in part because efforts occur outside of the discipline's sphere of professional influence. This disassociation may be a reflection of the diminished role of architecture and urbanism in the wake of the 1990s economic crisis or the government's rigid and limiting

A public path bifurcates an organopónico—it has been preserved for circulation despite the change in land use.

153

control of state-run design firms. These factors both impact the integration of design into urban agriculture efforts, preventing a more inclusive and holistic conception of the process.

Nevertheless, a number of architects and planners in Havana have taken an interest in the urban agriculture movement through personal research or have at least conceded that the informal allocation of city gardens impacts urban form in important ways. For instance, city historian Eusebio Leal Spengler, the esteemed and vocal force behind the multimillion dollar tourist industry resurrected in Old Havana, buffers unsightly food crops with flowers in organopónicos.[10] This is a striking example of what landscape architect and scholar Mira Engler calls a "camouflage approach" to landscape design, one that denies the aesthetic value of food production. In Havana, the few examples of formally designed farms use hedge and flower plantings to mask farming from the surrounding city.[11]

While the urban agriculture movement is widely supported by Cubans, many of these advocates today also support efforts to introduce more comprehensive planning and design into the urban farming movement. In contrast to the organic and ad-hoc form these gardens assumed during the early stages of the food crisis, people now see an opportunity to better relate the material, environmental, and social aspects of urban agriculture with other urban processes. In an effort to facilitate this transition, Havana's city government has incorporated urban agriculture into the city's land-management plans, adopting legislation and regulations that support and protect this work.[12] At the popular level, urban agriculture is now so visible and useful that it has a protected role in the city, both physically and culturally. Indeed, many Cubans see urban agriculture as a valued landscape type within the city of Havana, beyond the production of food and capital.[13]

The recognition of urban agriculture as a piece of the broader physical planning process paves the way for a more critical, integrated, and perhaps effective future role for agriculture in the city. Since 2000, urban agriculture has become a permanent type of land use in Havana's master plan. Access to land granted through usufruct has become increasingly flexible during the past five years, opening up new possibilities for people to qualify for loans, to co-opt idle land, and to have better long-term security on their farmland. Cuba's formalization of this city-planning strategy is a critical milestone, one that guarantees a place for this foodscape in a post–Special Period Havana. Thus the Cuban government has effectively legitimized urban agriculture—promoting it from a fringe movement pre-1989 to a valued economic driver and a central pillar of Cuban identity. This newfound status also provides other individuals and institutions—perhaps even designers—with the language and conceptual framework that they could use to effectively advocate for urban agriculture.[14]

While some specific urban design strategies have been employed to accommodate farming at the city scale, most of the post-crisis agricultural innovation parallels practices deployed throughout the country. In this respect, many of the farming practices in urban growing areas appear to simply be downsized versions of rural practices. Surprisingly, the inverse situation may also be true: Raúl Castro has appealed to rural farmers to "apply the same concepts of Urban Agriculture in traditional agriculture."[15] However, urban areas differ radically from their rural counterparts in size and shape, and these smaller footprints support more productive and diverse crops. With dense populations and dangerous environmental pollutants, cities also require more rigorous

155

Top: A typical bed, irrigation, and crop layout
Bottom: Recycled plastic bottles used as watering devices
on one rooftop

agricultural management to safeguard the health and safety of their growing areas. Current regulations in Havana ensure that plants and animals grown in low-tech enterprises are done so in accordance with human health and sanitation laws, but little oversight ensures compliance.

Without articulating a specific design form, Havana's current office of urban agriculture prescribes six design mandates: agroecology and sustainable agriculture; production diversity; small-scale crops for state, cooperative, and private groups; economic adequacy; preserving harmony with the urban environment; and preservation of the goals of the Revolution.[16] The state provides design guidelines that are technical rather than formal, describing how to orient beds for optimal solar access, where and how to plant trees and shrubs, and other pragmatic farming tips. The office of urban agriculture in Havana has developed a lengthy list of target goals, which include the following objectives for urban farms: processing and distributing food; reusing material resources; improving food security; increasing the amount of food available to the poor in urban areas; increasing access to fresh food; increasing the variety and nutritional value of available food; eliminating poverty by generating income and jobs; strengthening local economies; and converting underutilized vacant land or green space for productive uses. These administrators state that urban agriculture should contribute to human and environmental health, restore traditional farming methods and medicinal plants, and improve both soil and urban microclimates. Even in the absence of formal design goals, they provide broad program guidelines and standards that could lead the state to adopt a more holistic and cohesive design language.

These design goals and physical guidelines have been made available to farmers through the state's agricultural

support network in an effort to develop a countrywide urban farming vision. Very few design firms, however, have consulted on projects that implement these directives. Two notable designers, Maria Caridad Cruz and Jorge Peña Diaz, are working to repair this divide. They teach design principles of urban farming through two different state-based organizations, which may affect change in the perception of formally designed agricultural landscapes for a new generation of students.

New Natural Infrastructures

That urban farming emerged in almost every physical context in Havana is a testament to the flexibility of the movement's

Above: One of many remaining vacant lots that would be a valuable site for a farm *Opposite:* A farm employee builds new raised beds for vermiculture from cinder blocks

159

design, the tenacity of the Cuban growers, and the support of the Cuban government. These growing spaces are truly "architectural accretions, layerings of program and use, existing infrastructures made useful," in what landscape architect Chris Reed calls the "new civic realm, one created by appendage and insertion."[17] This creative space appropriation also points to a new form of ecological urbanism that American landscape theorists see as a critical platform for environmental stewardship. Landscape architect James Corner's assertion that "ecologically aligned landscape architects see cities as grossly negligent with regard to nature" may well be true, but in Havana, gardens serve useful ecological functions within the city that may begin to repair this divide.[18] Productive urban landscapes demand the theoretical reframing of outdated conceptions around the division of nature and the city. The infusion of productivity into this infrastructure also stands to recast urban landscapes, from what Corner calls "a bourgeois aesthetic" to something far more vital.[19] The pairing of landscapes of pleasure and of utility could link the living tissue of the city to urban needs and values, lot by vacant lot.

Havana's urban agriculture emerged as an infrastructural response rather than a set of discrete architectural interventions. Despite its organizational legibility, the city's farming system stems from unplanned and informal design decisions, with an aesthetic identity more in line with landscape urbanism than the disciplines of architecture and urban planning.[20] However, designers could contribute important ideas for the development and deployment of urban gardens, and, in doing so, could improve the relevance of their chosen profession. As Havana's economy opens up to the competing land uses of tourism and industrial production, urban farming will need to stake its claim on available land in the city.

NOTES

1. Mark Wigley, "Space in Crisis."
2. Ibid.
3. Cruz and Medina, *Agriculture in the City*, 178.
4. Keller Easterling, "Fresh Field," in *Pamphlet Architecture* 30, 10.
5. Premat, *Sowing Change*, 45.
6. Ibid., 26.
7. Ibid., 45.
8. Ibid., 27.
9. Jorge Peña Díaz, interview with the author, January 4, 2012.
10. Spengler adheres to the saying, "Where Go Flowers, Lettuce Should Not Go." Premat, *Sowing Change*, 108.
11. Mira Engler, "Designing America's Waste Landscapes," in *Large Parks*, 37.
12. These proactive state-sponsored developments include the opening of state lands for urban farming through usufruct rights, the delineation of food parks as a new land-use type, and provisions for the preservation of agricultural landscapes within the city limits.
13. Cruz and Medina, *Agriculture in the City*, 23.
14. Ibid., 171.
15. González et al., *Testimonios*, 105.
16. Ibid., 26.
17. Chris Reed, "Public Works Practice," in *The Landscape Urbanism Reader*, 282.
18. James Corner, "Terra Fluxus," in *The Landscape Urbanism Reader*, 27.
19. Ibid.
20. These design strategies correlate to the sub-practices of architecture identified by InfraNet Lab and Lateral Office as infrastructure's expanded field, including "productive surfaces, programmed containers, and civic conduits." Havana's urban farming system relies on all three. White et al., "Formatting Contingency," 8.

The Productive City

Jonathan Tate

A cultivated field amid the rich urban fabric of Havana is the clearest indicator of the noted food-production system that fuels this city. Neat, tended rows of seasonal vegetables nestled among high-rise housing embody a system that has been lauded as both a savior for a desperate population and a progressive hope for many other developed cities around the world. Equally as remarkable—though less picturesque—are the infrastructure pieces for this urban food system: strands of marketplaces, outposts for planting material and agriculture advice, and the organizations that monitor and regulate the system.

While now under the auspices of governmental authorities, this network of parts (production, selling, and education of new growers) is the consequence of an urban community responding to a food crisis and necessarily developing a system of self-sufficiency. The impact on the city through this capitalization of space fundamentally reshaped the physical environment. Plots of land, whether large interurban tracts or a small sliver of cultivatable space above or between buildings became opportunities for control over one's survival. In this sense the concept of productive urban space became visible: Farming presented a land use that engaged and activated unused or unrecognized terrain in the city. And the independent actions of growers fomented and guided this necessary form of agency.

The results offer an opportunity to reflect on the ways that this is emblematic of larger urban phenomena in global cities today. Specifically, this precedent illustrates the captivating ability of citizens to reinvent land use in response to pressing needs, creating new productive space within the city. On a broader level, urban farming functions as a device to activate swaths of fallow land, providing a potential for restoring urban space otherwise abandoned or neglected. As a conceptual act, this mode of engagement allows urbanists to reconsider and frame other inventive adaptations of contemporary urban space, either through human-made interventions or emergent natural processes. Collectively, these new productive infrastructures have the potential to redefine how we understand the city today.

Productive Plot

Farming within the city is not a new idea, given the historical inseparability of cultivation and urbanization. However, the formalization of the city and the expansion of its supportive hinterland established a precedent for the polarized relationship between agricultural production and the urban center. In today's globalized economic context, the path between manufactured objects (food or any other consumable item) and end users can be so complicated and abstract that it seems impossible to track. The Cuban urban farming model represents a recoupling of city life with the fundamentals that sustain it—regressing, perhaps, to a state of urban preorigination—while recognizing the potentials for production within its own framework.

The development of urban agricultural and collaborative farming models has only recently proliferated in the United States. While not born from crisis, this nevertheless reflects critical self-sufficiency. Whether as a response to the local food movement, community initiatives, or the simple desire to connect to one's food source, gardens have resurfaced in most cities today.

At this small scale, farming essentially reshapes our conception of land use in the city. The urban fabric is no longer conceived of as a singular space of social and commercial interaction but also supports sites for beneficial production. Cultivation—now in the lexicon of our urban frame of reference—has opened our understanding of the potentials for space to respond directly to our most basic human needs.

Raised beds and a storage shed at an organopónico

165

We can draw similar contextual relationships to the potential for farming in the impoverished urban districts called food deserts—the land of corner stores and processed, packaged foods, the parts of cities lacking access to fresh produce and healthy food items. In response, food-justice advocates frequently envision urban farm models for these areas, as a panacea to this problem. In this scenario, fallow land now would have the capacity to positively contribute—through productive cultivation—to the remaking of neighborhoods by addressing the nourishment of its residents.

Farming Vacancy

Even within the dense fabric of central Havana, opportunities for growing have been explored and exhausted. Rooftops, window planters, and errant slivers of land between sidewalks and walls have been appropriated for productive use. Outside of the central historic districts, vacant plots of land have been seized for more aggressive cultivation—occasionally in disregard of existing structures (physical, legal, or otherwise) already in place. In combination with the interurban tracts, these land groupings made possible the scale of cultivation necessary to feed the city.

As much as agriculture reconnects production with land use, it also reframes the possibilities for open urban space. In another incredible reversion, large farms that were subdivided to accommodate increasing urban populations are now being repurposed and reaggregated to provide space for planting. This produces an unexpected expression of a latent, historic condition, challenging expectations for vacant land in our cities. What it once was it is becoming again—this time with new insight and intention.

Reconceived as a viable land use for cities, urban farming is now a convenient planning tool to address another global phenomena: the economically repressed and depopulating city centers. The response to urban blight in cities ranging from Detroit to Leipzig has been to move the land into agricultural—and by extension economic—production writ large. Benevolent in conception and realization, agricultural plots offer quasi-pastoral, inexpensive repurposing of fallow sites, making them a palatable solution in the absence of traditional development. This provides not only a vehicle for sustenance but also a regenerative ointment for entire districts of underdeveloped or underutilized land. While a complicated and complex endeavor in terms of management, organization, and maintenance, the notion that a food-production system can take the place of bricks and mortar or a traditional park presents a significant conceptual shift. In Havana, this form of strategic development is also an accessible tool—not necessarily administered through professional or governmental services—and more often conceived and implemented from the ground up.

Invasive Urbanism

Perhaps the most alluring opportunity illuminated by Havana's agricultural phenomenon is the informal capitalization of land. Individuals—driven by a fragile economy—have seized vacant spaces in the city and exposed its latent potential, directly supporting plant growth for food production. Conceptually, however, this is emblematic of a new form of urban agency—protectively labeled here as invasive urbanism—aimed at exploiting hidden opportunistic conditions for supportive objectives, the effects of which result in the remaking of the city.

While the emphasis of the discussion of invasive urbanism has thus far been on urban agriculture—with its associated scales and types of engagement—the premise could easily be used to describe situations present elsewhere around the world.

In many rapidly urbanizing countries, for example, rural-urban migration-based population increases—among other pressures—overwhelm formal city structures and services, and self-initiated communities have become the de facto mode of development.

Informal settlements—perhaps the largest force of urban growth in developing countries today—are representative of these global trends. Housing is generated through adept, and often illegal, land seizure and the creative coupling of material and human resources. Replace the need for food with the

Vendors and customers at a market stand in Havana

need for housing, and the spatial agency underwriting each effort remains the same. The commonality between these two scenarios lies in the intentional codification of systemic thinking about how cities, driven by informal or invasive activities, can regenerate and evolve in the face of developmental pressures.

How do these precedents offer us a model or method with which we can develop our own urban environments? While most of these situations unfolded through invention, imagination, and informal tactics—and would not have existed otherwise— they nonetheless demonstrate opportunities for future formal development. As a starting point, planners and designers can help to support these natural outgrowths by providing the policy, space, tools, and ideas that people need to engage. These conditions can then provide the framework for development from which the future fabric of our cities can be intentionally molded.

In Havana, the success story of ground-up urban agriculture reveals the potential for other cities to be productive, generative tools that address real needs. This single, coordinated food-delivery system substantiated the multitude of constructive processes that exist and that can thrive within the city. With this striking precedent we can recognize how urban anomalies might inform natural systems and processes, human needs and attitudes toward space, and the consequences of economic and political actions. As we move forward, acute observations and adaptive responses—matching the inventiveness of extant conditions—may be our greatest design tool.

Moving
Forward

DESPITE MORE THAN TWO DECADES OF DEVELOPMENT, CUBA maintains what could euphemistically be called an open relationship with urban agriculture: The country imports approximately 84 percent of its food from abroad, and the ever-relaxing market restrictions under Raúl Castro may ultimately devalue the currency of local produce.[1] Many urban agriculture experts in Havana worry that Cuba's economic improvement "could give rise to the intensified use of [conventional agriculture] practices and undo the progress of achievements gained in this period of transition to more sustainable forms of urban and peri-urban agriculture."[2] Just as the widespread use of the bicycle that grew out of Cuba's oil shortages in the early 1990s quickly fell out of favor when vehicles became available again, urban farming could be viewed as a necessary chore not worth pursuing in a more comfortable economic climate.

A surprising discovery for visitors to Havana is that, despite the widespread propaganda advertising the urban farming movement, not every city surface is covered in edible plants. One might expect that all available landscapes would be necessarily appropriated for food production, but there are many other types of green spaces in Havana, including parks, ornamental gardens, and even suburban front yards. This stark reality denies visitors their utopian fantasies of perfectly productive urban landscapes, forces a more critical evaluation of the universal acceptability of urban agriculture, and may in fact point to a shift away from informal urban farming.

While Cuba's urban agriculture has been highlighted as a social movement stemming from the values of the Revolution, this patriotism does not illustrate how and why it first came into being. Havana's progressive and interconnected urban agriculture originated because people had no other choice than to self-provision, quite literally because urban dwellers were relentlessly hungry. Disassociated from the revolution, and well outside of the jurisdiction of the state, the practice of urban agriculture emerged "as a personal choice for survival in a context of uneven food access."[3] While this is not a desirable position for any society to begin an agricultural reform, it was the catalyst that initiated a new model for post-oil resilience and a blueprint for a more optimistic future.

For countries seeking to improve their food security, Havana's urban farming system offers an exciting new prototype, tested over decades on a shoestring budget. Agroecological education has led to more efficient and economical farming solutions, bolstering the country's food

A lush front yard in the Vedado

security while denouncing the Green Revolution and corporate agricultural practices of the past. The combination of artisanal pesticide labs, localized application of agricultural research, and an enormous network of engaged growers points to the country's investment in self-sufficient food production.

In a city that has historically lacked green space, the urban farming movement has ushered in a new layer of infrastructure. This transformation appears in physical, social, and political forms, altering urban space and impacting the livability of the city. Some 13 percent of all food produced in Cuba comes from cities and towns, and close to 100 percent of the leafy greens consumed in Havana are produced inside city limits.[4] Affordable, semiorganic, city-grown produce has become ubiquitous in Havana, and residents celebrate this achievement.

The Cuban agricultural system also provides a successful model for other countries to follow. Havana's urban farming movement has two fundamental components: It is functional—an effective response to acute food shortages and the real issue of hunger—and it is ideological—promoting the socialist values of peasant work, whether in the fields or on the rooftop. The lessons from Cuba are relevant today, and as this state-supported growing infrastructure does not require a catalytic crisis to be effective, its story provides an accessible narrative that other countries could appropriate. As demonstrated in Cuba's agricultural recovery, urban food systems perform surprisingly well, particularly when implemented as an iterative process moving in the direction of radical self-sufficiency.

Designing for the Future City

In the United States, corporate agribusiness promotes a food system that favors monoculture, reliance on chemical fertilizers and pesticides, and seemingly unsustainable transportation structures. This form of agriculture also reflects a political system that subsidizes unsustainable and inequitable modes of national food provisioning. What, then, are the alternatives? Could urban design engagement bend corporate-agriculture interests, political will, and community relationships toward healthier agricultural practices and access to food? Might new designs for farming and food distribution actually foster more democratic and equitable social relationships? Cuba's urban farming approach suggests a compelling alternative to the U.S. system and offers up its quarter-century-old experimental urban landscape for study.

If design is to play a part in the transition to more sustainable food landscapes, then the design profession will need to expand to include broader terms and a more collaborative approach. By framing this conversation around landscape urbanism, designers could shift their focus from radical form-making to responsive design moves, which are ultimately more fluid in both approach and engagement over time. In the team-based redesign of a food system, physical outcomes might be less useful to the urban agriculture project than a well-designed framework. With a truly interdisciplinary and collaborative team, front-end design guidance might launch the urban food movement into greater efficacy, accessibility, and legibility.

Regardless of the role of designers, incorporating urban agriculture into the development of the future city requires that citizens attend to urban landscapes and become comfortable with a living, breathing infrastructure. It is likely too that this redesign will favor the local: "localism is, however, more likely to be the required modus operandi for the post peak-oil world, just as globalism was for the cheap-oil era."[5] In greening the urban hardscape and reestablishing locavore foodsheds, urban farming initiatives also ensure the sustainability of these practices. The innovation, creative reuse, and culture of sharing and helping that resulted in

Cuba's urban agriculture could have successful outcomes in other places as well. In the case of cities in transition, lessons learned from this methodology come without the strain of crisis and help to suggest a way forward without the burden of catastrophe.

Translating Cuban Innovation to Other Regions

Urbanists promote local agriculture because it greens the city, increases the productivity of underused spaces, creates jobs, provides stronger links between farms and tables, supports community engagement and interaction, and improves urban resilience. The resurrection of Havana's local foodshed stands

A farmer looks after a merliton vine at his parcela.

Honey harvest, with frames of honeycomb
pulled from hives

out as an elegant and sophisticated response to a problem that many other countries share. Moreover, it stands out as a useful model for other industrialized nations, as it has been tested within a heavily developed urban area, similar in form and scale to many contemporary global cities.

Cuba is far from utopian: The country continues to lose population to emigration and defends policies that deny citizens basic human rights, such as the freedom of speech. Because of the nature of Cuba's political leadership, many of the agricultural programs that have flourished on the island might flounder under other less autocratic forms of government. This also suggests that strong government was a critical factor in Havana's astonishing capacity for food production. Nevertheless, urban farming underscores many universal aspirations for community improvement, such as self-sufficiency, health, affordable produce, and food security, and lessons from Cuba could be readily retooled for other regions.

There is good evidence that Cuba's brand of urban agriculture—organized, pervasive, and subsidized—could translate well to other places. Many parallel programs are already underway: Alice Waters's wildly successful Edible Schoolyard Project—which was initiated in Berkeley and has spread to other U.S. cities, such as New Orleans—for instance, looks a lot like a school-based autoconsumo. Greening of Detroit, an organization that assists some sixteen hundred growers, supports urban agriculture in the patios and parcelas of Motown. While this nonprofit estimates that their growers currently produce just 2 percent of the city's fresh food, they have also spearheaded the development of larger, more profitable market gardens— not unlike Havana's organopónicos—to help bridge this gap.[6]

In Havana, urban agriculture has had a profound impact on neighborhood functioning and aesthetics. Vacant lots once linked to garbage, disease, and crime now *generate* health and have changed people's attitudes about public space. Peter Rosset sees the Cuban model as an important and viable one for other global cities, where urban agriculture interventions could simply act "to restore hope for many urban and suburban dwellers in many countries."[7] Of course, many U.S. cities do not support urban farming because this practice is considered an unsuitable—or even wasteful—use of urban resources. According to critics, urban agriculture competes for valuable land, presents public-health risks by bringing animals and organic products into cities, comingles food with polluted soils, and taxes land and water resources. Proponents of large-scale corporate agribusiness will simply suggest that the piecemeal approach of urban farming exhibited in Havana lacks the efficiency and economy of consolidated agricultural efforts.

Regardless, urban agriculture is one of the many ways that people shape their cities, and it demonstrates a direct and proactive approach to building urban resilience. To allow for this type of land use is to support a form of engaged citizenship, what geographer David Harvey articulates as the "right to change and reinvent the city more after our heart's desire."[8] Sociologist and educator Diane Davis suggests that this civilian buy-in is also a key factor in rebuilding after crisis, where "recovery—and perhaps even resiliency—also has to do with establishing legitimacy, which means understanding and responding in some fashion to the priorities that citizens hold for their city."[9] Urban farming—whether born out of crisis or a planning process—may work principally because it is powered by engaged citizens. Moreover, their efforts point to a growing interest in participatory urbanism, and the value that these interventions can bring to public space in any country.

NOTES

1. Carmelo Mesa Lago, "La economía de Cuba hoy: Retors internos y externos," *Desarollo Economíco* 49, no. 195 (2009): 421-50.
2. Cruz and Medina, *Agriculture in the City*, 195.
3. Premat, *Sowing Change*, 55.
4. This statistic came from the National Institute for Fruits and Tropical Research (ILIEFAT) whose numbers are not reliable due to strong incentives for government agencies to report highly positive outcomes.
5. Newman, Beatley, and Boyer, *Resilient Cities*, 156.
6. Ashley Atkinson, interview with author, 2012.
7. González et al., *Testimonios*, 126.
8. Harvey, *Rebel Cities*, 4.
9. Diane Davis, "Reverberations, Mexico City's 1985 Earthquake and the Transformation of Capital," in *The Resilient City*, 266-67.

After-
word

IT CAN BE TEMPTING FOR AN AMERICAN TO FETISHIZE CUBA.
Iconic images popularly associated with Cuba reinforce a
caricature of the nation, and in both the United States and
Cuba, propaganda can be outrageously misleading, with official
documents reinforcing state goals and values. Moving beyond
the biases held by these countries and their citizens has been
increasingly challenging due to their imposed travel restrictions.

In an effort to provide an impartial account of Havana's
urban farming landscape, I interviewed many different stakeholders
with distinct perspectives. I logged many field hours, in an effort
to gain firsthand experience of the physical farms and spaces.
Havana's urban-food movement has a diverse pool of participants,
including professors, city planners, architects, educators,
permaculture leaders, government agronomists, filmmakers,
journalists, and thousands of farmers and growers. Despite personal
risk, as the dissemination of this information is controlled by
the government, many freely shared their experiences and
resources: stories, articles, data, maps, photographs, and drawings.

Cuba is changing. During the course of this research,
the government has loosened market restrictions as icy U.S.
attitudes gradually thaw. The country's marketplace is undergoing
rapid shifts under the new leadership of Raúl Castro; more
products and tools have become available to growers, including
technologies and building materials that allow for advances
in farming techniques. The food crisis responsible for creating
the robust urban-farming movement has now stabilized, and
citizens are shifting their focus to long-term goals of resilience and
stewardship. It is reassuring then that, as the program evolves,
Cuba's brand of urban agriculture remains at the forefront of
the global food-justice movement, carrying with it the next wave
of audacious experiments.

Appendix

A. Monthly Ration

10 eggs
 5 lbs rice
 2 lbs sugar
 ½ lb black beans
 1 package of salt every 3 months
 4 oz of coffee/chicory mix
 ½ liter oil
 1 tube of toothpaste

In addition, children under the age of seven qualify for milk, and people with approved dietary constraints—such as diabetes or high cholesterol—qualify for slight adjustments in the ration. No vegetables or fruit are provided in the ration, but they are available at subsidized prices in state-run markets and at free markets in Havana.

Per person, per month, unless otherwise stated, circa January 2013.

B. Typical Products

Viandas: sweet potato, plantain, yucca, squash, yams

Vegetables: Chinese cabbage, beans, lettuce, cucumber, plantain, tomato, okra, beet, turnip, carrots, potatoes, onions, garlic, peppers

Cooking herbs: parsley, oregano, thyme

Grains: maize, rice, taro

Medicinal herbs: taro tubers, lemongrass, mint, chamomile

Flowers: aster, sunflowers, gladiolus, marigold

Tree saplings: timber, fruit, hedge

Meat: cows, pigs, poultry, horses, oxen, goats, sheep, rabbits

Fruits: avocado, guava, lemon, coconut, orange, lime, pineapple, mango

Milk: goat, cow

Other: honey, soil, seeds

C. Agricultural Groups

ACAO: Cuban Organic Agriculture Association, now called the Organic Farming Group (GAO)

ACPA: Cuban Association of Animal Production

ACTAF: Cuban Association of Agricultural and Forestry Technicians

ANAP: National Association of Small Farmers

CCS: Credit and Service Cooperatives

CDR: Committees for the Defense of the Revolution

CENPALAB: National Center for Laboratory Animal Production

CENSA: National Center for Agricultural Health

CIMA: Animal Improvement Research Center

COMECON: Council for Mutual Economic Assistance

CREE: Center for Entomophages and Entomopathogens

ECICC: Coffee and Cocoa Central Research Station

ENPA: National Agricultural Projects Company

ETP: Directorate of Technical Education and Vocational (within the MINED)

FANJNH: Antonio Núñez Jiménez Foundation for Nature and Man

FMC: Federation of Cuban Women

GAO: Organic Farming Group, formerly called the Cuban Organic Agriculture Association (ACAO)

GDIC: Holistic Development of the Capital Group

GNAU: National Group for Urban Agriculture

ICA: Institute of Animal Science

IIA: Poultry Research Institute

IIF: Forest Research Institute

IIFT: Research Institute of Tropical Fruit

IIHLD: Horticultural Research Institute Liliana Dimitrova

IIP: Swine Research Institute

IIRD: Research Institute of Irrigation and Drainage

IMV: Institute of Veterinary Medicine

INCA: National Institute of Agricultural Sciences

INIFAT: Research Institute for Tropical Agriculture Alexander von Humboldt

INISAV: Research Institute of Plant Protection

INRE: National Institute of State Reserve

IS: Land Institute

MES: Ministry of Higher Education

MINAG: Ministry of Agriculture (also MINAGRI)

MINED: Ministry of Education

MINFAR: Ministry of the Revolutionary Armed Forces

PDS-CIC: Sustainable Development Program of the Council of Churches of Cuba

PDVSA: Venezuelan Petroleum SA

SNTAF: National Union of Agriculture and Forestry

UBPC: Basic Units of Cooperative Production

UNAH: Agrarian University of Havana

Contributors

CAREY CLOUSE teaches architecture and urbanism at the University of Massachusetts Amherst and practices architecture for disaster resilience with Crookedworks Architecture. Her professional work and research addresses the intersection of design and sustainability, with a specific focus on food security and self-sufficiency.

ANDREW COOK is a photographer based in Cambridge, Massachusetts. He holds a BFA from Cooper Union and has lived and worked extensively in Baltimore and New Orleans. His work focuses on the people and ideas behind innovative urban-food culture.

FRITZ HAEG's work includes edible gardens, public dances, educational environments, animal architecture, domestic gatherings, urban parades, temporary encampments, documentary videos, publications, exhibitions, Web sites, and, occasionally, buildings for people. Recent projects include Edible Estates, a series of public domestic edible gardens located internationally; Animal Estates, a housing initiative for native wildlife in cities around the world, which debuted at the 2008 Whitney Biennial; and the Sundown Schoolhouse, an itinerant educational program.

JADE JIAMBUTR is an architectural intern and graphic designer living in New York. He graduated from Tulane University with a master of architecture in 2012.

ZACHARY LAMB is an urban-rebuilding professional, designer, and educator, pursuing a PhD in planning at MIT. He received a master of architecture from MIT and a BA from Williams College. He has taught architecture classes at Tulane University and international design-build courses at MIT. He currently undertakes research, design, and construction projects with Crookedworks Architecture.

JORGE PEÑA DIAZ is a professor of architecture and the former dean of the FAH Architecture School in Havana, as well as the former head of the Center for Urban Studies of Havana. He addresses issues relating to architecture, urbanism, and the environment with the Urban Research and Action group at the Center for Urban Studies of Havana. He also collaborates with the National Commission on Culture, Cities, and Architecture; the task force for Havana's urban development update; the COST Action Urban Agriculture Europe project, supported by the European Union; the Urban Atlas of Havana; and the America program of the Escola da Cidade in São Paulo, Brazil.

JONATHAN TATE is a professor at Tulane School of Architecture and a principal at Office of Jonathan Tate (OJT). His research includes investigations on opportunistic urban developments— informal settlements, ecologic anomalies, etc.—and their spatial and cultural implications. His work with OJT and previous work with other offices include a wide variety of project and program types, both rural and urban, which have been published nationally and internationally.

Acknowledgments

Contributors: Jorge Peña Diaz, Fritz Haeg, Zachary Lamb, and Jonathan Tate

Artwork: Andy Cook (photographs) and Jade Jiambutr (drawings)

Support: Kenneth Schwartz, Tulane School of Architecture; Elisabeth Hamin, Stephen Schreiber, and the Faculty Research Grant Fund at the University of Massachusetts Amherst

At Princeton Architectural Press: Meredith Baber, Linda Lee, and Jennifer Lippert.

On the Ground: Amandla, Angel-Luis, Aquiles, Aurelia, Carídad, Carlos, Caryn, Catherine, Charles, Dave, Ethan, Fernando, Fernando Senior, Hector, Isis, Ivonne, Jaspar, Jess, Johanna, Jonathan, Juan, Laura Len, Mario, Nelson, Rainer, Raul, and Vickie.

All royalties from the sale of this book will be donated to the Grow Dat Youth Farm.

Published by
Princeton Architectural Press
37 East Seventh Street
New York, New York 10003

Visit our website at www.papress.com.

Editor: Meredith Baber
Designer: Elana Schlenker

All photography by Andrew Cook
All graphic artwork by Jade Jiambutr

Special thanks to: Mariam Aldhahi, Sara Bader, Janet Behning, Nicola Brower,
Megan Carey, Carina Cha, Andrea Chlad, Barbara Darko, Benjamin English, Russell Fernandez,
Will Foster, Jan Haux, Diane Levinson, Jennifer Lippert, Katharine Myers, Jaime Nelson,
Lauren Palmer, Rob Shaeffer, Sara Stemen, Andrew Stepanian, Marielle Suba, Paul Wagner,
and Joseph Weston of Princeton Architectural Press —Kevin C. Lippert, publisher

Library of Congress Cataloging-in-Publication Data

Clouse, Carey, 1979–
Farming Cuba : urban farming from the ground up / Carey Clouse.—First edition.
     pages cm
Other title: Urban farming from the ground up
Includes bibliographical references.
ISBN 978-1-61689-200-5 (alk. paper)
1. Urban agriculture—Cuba. 2. Landscape design—Cuba. I. Title. II. Title: Urban farming from
the ground up.
S477.C82C56 2014
635.9'77097291—dc23
                                                        2013029565